The Whisper of Christmas

Reflections for
Advent and
Christmas

Joe E. Pennel, Jr.

The Upper Room
Nashville, Tennessee

The Whisper of Christmas

Scripture quotations not otherwise identified are from the Revised Standard Version of the Bible, copyrighted 1946, 1952, and © 1971 by the Division of Christian Education, National Council of the Churches of Christ in the United States of America, and are used by permission.

Any scripture passage designated AP is the author's paraphrase.

Book Design: Harriette Bateman
Cover Transparency: John Netherton
Second Printing: June, 1986 (5)
Library of Congress Catalog Number: 84-50839
ISBN 0-8358-0492-5

Printed in the United States of America

To Janene, my wife
To Melanie and Heather, my daughters
    For helping me to experience what is
    love.

Contents

Acknowledgments

I am indebted to my exceedingly efficient and dedicated secretary, Miss Iris Groomes, for patient and painstaking typing and retyping of the manuscript; to Mrs. Mary Ann Haney, her faithful assistant; to Mrs. Janice Grana and Mrs. Charla Honea for editorial assistance; and to Dr. Rueben Job, World Editor of The Upper Room, for proposing that I write this book.

The Whisper of Christmas could not have been written had it not been for those seen and unseen influences which have shaped my thoughts. To that host of great minds and spirits, I express my profound gratitude.

Finally, I am grateful to my wife, Janene, and my two daughers, Melanie and Heather, for foregoing many of the family rituals of an ordinary Advent and Christmas in order that this book might be completed.

Preface

I wrote *The Whisper of Christmas* because I felt that God had a bone to pick with me. For years I have complained about the lack of resources for the liturgical season of Advent and Christmas. My rather persistent discontent finally led me to write something about the meaning of Advent and Christmastide rather than lament over the absence of material.

The words of this book were written between Sundays, pastoral visits, meetings, appointments, funerals, weddings, conferences, and all that intervenes in the life and work of a pastor. They were written in my study, on the kitchen table, while sitting in an overstuffed recliner, in flight, and wherever a quiet place could be located. They were often penned on the run and on paper of every sort and size. Most of all, this book was written while I interacted with the people of my congregation during Advent and Christmas. This document was enriched by the experiences of a church as that congregation was nourished by the symbols, meanings, and feelings of this significant season.

The chapters speak of Advent as waiting, repentance, hope, and expectation. The daily reflections included in four of the chapters are my musings about God's Advent among the children of God.

The Whisper of Christmas may not change your life dramatically, but if it deepens your commitment to the meaning of Advent and Christmas, it will have been worth the effort. I have written this book with the prayer that the story of "then" and "there" can become the story for "here" and "now."

Introduction

There is a time for everything. *The Whisper of Christmas* is written for a very important time called *Advent* and *Christmas.*

It can be read by keeping time with the season. That is to say, the reader can use this book as a spiritual resource for each Sunday and each day of the Advent and Christmas season. The Sunday readings develop the major themes which are uniquely related to that particular day. The daily reflections are intended to help the reader reflect upon life from the vantage point of the Christian faith. Following the Fourth Sunday in Advent there are no daily reflections. Instead, there are major readings for Christmas Eve and Christmas Day which the reader may wish to reflect upon throughout the week.

The Whisper of Christmas can also be read as any other book: at one sitting or from time to time. Since the chapters and daily reflections are free-standing, the reader may choose what portions to read when.

The book can also be used by church school classes, sharing groups, prayer groups, and study groups as a basis for seasonal study and reflection. If used in this way, the Sunday chapters could become the focus for serious group study while the daily reflections could provide a resource for individuals on a daily basis. Clergy, teachers, and group leaders can also use *The Whisper of Christmas* as source material for sermons and lessons.

This book, like Advent and Christmas, provides many options for hearing the whisper that is in this holy season.

The Whisper of Christmas

First Week in Advent

This is the testimony of John, when the Jews
sent priests and Levites from Jerusalem to ask
him, "Who are you?" He confessed, he did not deny,
but confessed, "I am not the Christ." And they
asked him, "What then? Are you Elijah?" He said,
"I am not." "Are you the prophet?" And he answered,
"No." They said to him then, "Who are you? Let
us have an answer for those who sent us. What
do you say about yourself?" He said, "I am the voice
of one crying in the wilderness, 'Make straight
the way of the Lord,' as the prophet Isaiah said."
Now they had been sent from the Pharisees.
They asked him, "Then why are you baptizing, if
you are neither the Christ, nor Elijah, nor the
prophet?" John answered them, "I baptize with
water; but among you stands one whom you do
not know, even he who comes after me, the thong
of whose sandal I am not worthy to untie." This
took place in Bethany beyond the Jordan, where
John was baptizing.

—John 1:19–28

John Netherton

Sunday: Waiting

As a child, I remember that the most difficult part of Christmas was simply waiting for it to arrive. From Thanksgiving to December 25 seemed more like an eternity than a month. Days seemed like weeks. Weeks felt like seasons. Time seemed to stand still.

Waiting is foreign to those of us who are accustomed to moving in the fast lane. Waiting seems unnatural. Knowing how to wait is, at best, an uncommon trait. We hunger for immediate satisfaction. The idea of delayed gratification is a stranger to our thinking.

Our society is alive with the symbols of our unwillingness or inability to wait. Exquisite taste does not sell TV dinners. Not having to prepare a meat-and-two-vegetable dinner is what makes this fare popular. Prepackaged vegetables in sealed bags are popular because they can easily be dropped in a 1½-quart pan of boiling water. Fast-food chains are booming because we can move through a little, crooked line, call out an order, sit down, eat, and rush on to the next lap of the rat race.

Condensed books are popular with busy people who do not have the patience to work through interesting sentence structure, innuendo, and the implications and subtleties of a great work. Time must be saved for greater responsibilities!

Many kitchens house Mr. Coffee machines; one simply spoons in the coffee and pours in water. The coffee is made before a cup can be found. In making the coffee this way, however, we miss the full "brew" of it. The rich aroma of the coffee does not drift through the house and into our nostrils as it did when it was perked or steeped. We give up the brew and the aroma in order to have it quickly.

People no longer want to dine. The leisurely meal, good conversation, and soft music are sacrificed for fast service, the check, the tip—and all because of busy schedules.

I can accept much of our no-wait approach to modern life, but I cannot bear instant potatoes. I like my potatoes baked until I can dress the soft white substance with hunks of butter and golf-ball-sized scoops of sour cream. I like to stir in the fixings until the steaming spud is ready to complement the entire meal. Instant potatoes cannot match that.

Waiting is difficult for modern people. We become ill, and we want to be made well now and not later. Medications, physicians, pastoral care, and love are often rejected if they are not swift. We want a miracle drug, the right prescription, and the best surgeon so that we can suddenly be back to our hurried routines. Six weeks out of seventy-five years is a low percentage of sick time to healthy time, but we must recover immediately because we do not know how to wait.

Though we do not like to wait, waiting is part of living. For example, we wait for peace. I might someday wait for my son-in-law to come home from Lebanon or Nicaragua. My mother waited for her brother to come home from World War II. My great-grandmother waited for her son to come home from World War I. Our forefathers and mothers have waited for tired, tattered soldiers to come home from Cuba, the Spanish War, the Civil War, the War of 1812, and the American Revolution.

For centuries believers and nonbelievers have

had to live while waiting for something: peace, daylight, the recovery of sanity, or the coming of food stamps. Standing in line is commonplace. We have waited for a pass, a friend, a break, a payday, quitting time, death, the installments to be paid out, the family physician to come, prosperity, independence, comfort, the restoration of health, power, the Republicans to get in so the Democrats can get out, stocks to rise and fall, and the mailman. Waiting is not an option. It is part of living.

At the hospital, we pace in front of a swinging door marked "surgery." We wait for what is not yet, but for what is to be (or not to be). Living and waiting go hand in hand.

A colleague of mine recently learned that she was pregnant. Two days later she had signs of aborting the tiny fetus. Her physician assigned her to bed for twenty-four hours and said, "Wait." She said, "All I can do is wait. I feel helpless, as if the jury is out."

Waiting is like living in the meantime. It is like knowing but not knowing. It is *how* one waits that matters.

God's clock is wound a different way. Time is different. Waiting, not hurrying, is one of God's characteristics. This waiting God often tells the human that waiting is the appropriate posture.

Many years before the birth of Jesus, the Old Testament prophets were writing and talking about waiting for one who would be like a light for the darkness. Those to whom they spoke were weary with impatience. They wanted the Messiah *now.* They yearned for God to be on their clock. For years added to more years, through the events of history, through priests and poets, God said, "Wait."

That same note is sounded in the prologue of John's Gospel. Those who gave ear to the preaching of John the Baptist heard him say, "I am not the light, but I come to tell you about the light that is yet to come" (John 1:8, AP). Dissatisfied with his lack of urgency, the listeners pressed him to say more, but John could only say, "I am not he." So anxious were they for a Messiah that the masses tried to crown John the Baptist as the Messiah. Again, God's message was "wait."

I am writing these words during the first week in December, a time designated by the church as Advent. Advent, a season of four Sundays, opens the church year. Traditionally, the season begins on the Sunday closest to St. Andrew's Day, November 30. History tells us that the observance of Advent originated in France during the fifth century. The duration of the season varied from four to seven weeks until Pope Gregory I, the Bishop of Rome in the sixth century, set the season at four weeks. In those earlier days Advent was strictly observed: every Christian was required to attend church services and to fast daily.

The word *Advent* comes from the Latin word *advenire* (to come to). Advent's message is that God in Christ is coming to the world. This coming may be a past experience. God did come in Christ at Christmas. The prophets' promise was fulfilled in the Babe. This coming may also be a present experience. God may come to you this Christmas as a rebirth, either for the first time or as a renewed birth in the deeper regions of your being.

The Advent season, a period of four Sundays before Christmas Day, is a time of waiting for the Christian. This is an awkward season because it is most difficult for us to focus on the preliminary dimensions of the Christmas story. We had much rather go directly to Bethlehem without hearing anew the words of the prophets or John the Baptist.

Advent does not give us permission to rush to the manger. It says "wait."

The mood of Advent is expressed in the liturgical color violet. The paraments of the sanctuary and the stoles of clergy are purple, depicting a feeling of quiet dignity, royalty, and repentance. Violet once was the traditional color of a king's robe. This color is used by the church to signal the coming of Christ who is the King of kings. Advent, a time of waiting, is a time of solemn and sober thought about one's need of repentance. It provides a quiet time for watching, waiting, and praying for a new experience of Christ's birth.

Advent is a time of solemnity and sobriety. Traditionally, Advent is a penitential season, originally known as the "Winter Lent." This mood of sobriety is expressed not only in the liturgical color, purple, but in the music of Advent hymns such as "O Come, O Come, Emmanuel" and "Come, Thou Long-Expected Jesus." In some parts of Christendom choirs omit processionals or have "silent processionals." Weddings are often discouraged. Decorations and things festive are often delayed until Christmas Eve.

Advent stresses not so much fulfillment as the anticipation of fulfillment: Christ is about to be born in the cradle of the believer's heart and life. As a family looks forward to a son returning from a war or a bride anticipates her wedding day, so a Christian looks forward with joy to Christ's coming. Yet, this is a different kind of joy—a joy of hope amid solemnity. It is the quiet joy of anticipation.

One way to wait during Advent is to look with a blank stare as if one does not know what to expect. One of the distinct pleasures of my life was to serve a rural parish for six years. There are still some things that I miss: the earthy humor, the genuine warmth of the people, the lack of pretense, and the simple but real faith.

Late one chilly fall day, a farmer called me to the parsonage door and said, "Preacher, are you doing anything tonight?" "Just going to read for awhile," I said. He then politely invited me to go with a group of farmers to a cattle auction. Having been reared in a large southern city, I had never witnessed a stock sale. My curiosity ebbed and flowed as we drove fifty miles across winding roads to a huge auction barn. The inside of the windy barn, the strange smells, and the constant clatter were new for me.

For two long hours I sat there with an empty stare. I waited, but I could not interpret the activity. As cattle paraded, the bidders were anxious, whispering, taking notes, raising and lowering hands, nodding, waving, pointing, clapping, and calling. I was not involved in the process, because I did not appreciate or understand the process.

There is a different kind of waiting when I watch my daughter play with her school basketball team. I arrive at the gym early so I can smell the popcorn, watch the players warm up, and chat with the fans. Even before the tip-off, the game starts churning and moving inside my bones. It gets down inside of me, and I get inside of it, and we are at one with each other. Excitement begins to surge because I know something of what to anticipate.

There are two ways to wait during Advent. Some will wait with a hollow stare. Others will wait with anticipation. Knowing how to wait and where to look for Christ's coming is essential for the Advent season. People will look for Christ in a variety of places at this Advent. Some will look for his presence in the quiet visit of an old friend. Others will look for a sign of his coming in the reading of scripture, the thrill of a great novel, the majestic rhythm of an ageless poem, or in the sights, sounds, and symbols of congregational worship. Knowing how to wait and where to look is like a prelude to Messiah's birth.

About midafternoon on a gray Christmas Eve, I trudged to the county jail to visit one of my parishioners who had been incarcerated for robbing a restaurant called Corned-Beef House. The robbery occurred on the very night that his wife had given birth to their first child. He could see no way to reconcile his lack of money with the great need that he faced as a new father. After finishing a second cup of lukewarm coffee, he impulsively took $42.50 from the cashier. For his action, he was sentenced to fifteen years in prison by the state of Tennessee.

When I went for that Christmas Eve visit he was awaiting trial in the county jail. We sat in the visitors' gallery with a thick, mesh screen between us. While others were going through the rituals of preparing for Christmas Eve, I listened to him as he recounted the story of his life. He told what it was like to live in the "project," to have an invalid father, to live on the income of a mother who worked in a corner bakery, to fall in love, and to have a son. He also spoke about what it felt like to be a criminal, to await hearings, and to survive in a "hell hole" on Christmas Eve. He groped for the words that would illustrate his dread, disappointment, and despair. The tone of his voice, the tears in his eyes, the anxiety of his laughter told both of us that life, for him, was out of focus. As we touched fingers between the wire, I said, "Christ be with you." "And with you," he responded in a whisper.

Reflections flooded my mind as I motored home late that afternoon. How did the message of Christmas fit into the life situation that I had just experienced? What, indeed, was the Incarnation for a situation like this? Those questions and many others darted in and out of my mind as I drove up my driveway. Then I saw a car that belonged to two of our very dear friends.

As I walked into the den of our home, my friend came over and gave me a big bear hug and whispered "Merry Christmas" in my left ear.

On that Christmas Eve there were two "comings" of Christ: one in the voice of a convict in his cell and the other through a friend who reached out with the love and care of Christ.

If I had rushed to the manger, I would not have met God during the wait.

Daily Reflections

Monday: The Most Important Gift

I am pained by the realization that I have not yet purchased ninety percent of the gifts that I want to give this Christmas. Gift lists, for me, are always a bit difficult to balance.

I have been puzzling about what might be the most important gift that we can give. Might it be something expensive like a dainty piece of carefully crafted jewelry? Or something enlightening like one of those read-to-be-reread books? Possibly something beautiful like an original work of art? Maybe a small luxury like cashmere socks? What about a piece of handwork which reflects a profound labor of love? Why not consider something practical like a calendar? Or what about a gift certificate? Possibly a gift which requires very little effort like a note inside a Christmas card stating in some clever way that the gift will be forthcoming? Or an easy-to-exchange gift because we know the receiver already has one? But time is running out and we have to produce a "little something."

In addition to those tangible things we give at this season of giving, possibly, just possibly, there is something more we need to offer. At times it is far less difficult to give "things" than to give the most important gift—ourselves.

It is possible to give "things" without loving, but it is impossible to love without giving some part of ourselves.

27

Tuesday: The Meeting

It happened as I took my mother to the Greyhound Bus Station for her return trip home. I noticed one of those shaggy, offbeat characters bearing a sign which said, "Prepare to meet thy God." I have made fun of people and signs like that. They have made me angry and have made me chuckle in almost the same breath. Cartoonists have had a field day with these odd people and their odd statements.

As this year's version of Advent gets underway, I have a different feeling about even the most grotesque of these "Prepare to meet thy God" signs. If we ponder these words for a moment, they are indeed splendid. For God is precisely the One I want to meet at this Advent.

If we pass through Advent and do not have this "meeting" with the God who came in Christ, something essential will be missing from our lives as believers.

Preparing to meet God is exactly what we are preparing to do.

Wednesday: Another Reality

We have almost lost our sense of darkness. We can hardly imagine a dark village, a dark city street, a dark lane, or a dark monastery. By the same token, alas, we have lost a sensitive appreciation for that which light reveals.

We have made silence almost unknown; hence, we cannot comprehend the greatest of late medieval sounds, the singing of choirs and the ringing of church bells.

Moreover, our mobility has robbed us of our sense of place and station in the world. We, therefore, feel isolated and without roots. We can scarcely conceive of a time when each district, even each town, spoke a dialect or accent of its own.

It is even more difficult for us to imagine a time when the church and world were not so neatly separated.

In all of the shifting we have sustained a great loss. Our sense of awe and mystery has faded. That which we have given up may be far greater than what we have gained.

In the midst of these realities, what statement does Advent make about *another* reality?

Thursday: Is the World Too Strong for Us?

I hear it often. It is usually said with a chuckle or a half-grin: "Be careful what you say, the minister is here." If I am playing golf, my opponent will say, "Well, Joe, you have got the edge." No one, I feel, really means anything derogatory by these remarks, but underneath the comments something important is being said.

It is not uncommon for a well-meaning parishioner to tell me what it is like in the "real" world, as if I live in a different kind of world. "Out there in the real world," a layperson muttered, "there is more dirt than sugar." Or as one person recently put it: "If you worked in the real world, you would not feel as you do." My experience with life is not confined to the pulpit on Sunday morning. Like you, I read the paper, watch TV, make business deals, invest money, fuss with my children, get angry, become lonely, enjoy sports, get cheated, buy groceries, pay a house note, make love, and worry about my responsibility to my vocation. I also try to tend to the needs of people, because my business is people. In addition to being in and around the church building, you will find me standing by a death bed, visiting a home where there is a broken marriage, listening to the needs of the poor, administering a large congregation, visiting in psychiatric wards and drug treatment centers, helping to make referrals for a person who has lost his business, taking on some community issue, listening to a troubled youth.

That is the real world in which we *all* live. In many ways the world is too strong for us. Sometimes we feel overwhelmed. Advent, a time when we reflect on the coming of God in Christ, provides us the opportunity to regain our strength and hope.

Friday: Living Together

As we move through Advent ("Christ's coming"), we, as Christians, are aware of those areas of our personal and social life where Christ has not yet come. His absence is often dramatized by our attitudes and in our relationships with other human beings.

Our belief in Emmanuel ("God with us") causes the Christian conscience to be disturbed by bigotry or discrimination. I am troubled by the apparent rise in racism and anti-Semitism in the fabric of our society. I am saddened by the discrimination against elderly people, poor people, and people with handicapping conditions. As persons who follow the way of life as lived out by the Prince of Peace, it is important for us to say a firm and clean "No" to such attitudes and behavior.

It is also important to go beyond statements. In my opinion all churches and synagogues must mount vigorous programs of ethical education. More intentional efforts in our homes could be devoted to the ethical education of children and youth, particularly in the areas of brotherhood/sisterhood, race relations, and interfaith relations. Our future as a community, nation, and world is dependent, in large part, on our ability to live together with mutual respect for each other despite our differences.

Those who either subtly or overtly polarize, discriminate, and put down others contradict the life-giving spirit of Jesus who came to bring peace on earth and goodwill among all people. When we lend our support to peace and goodwill, we open ourselves to the possibility of a real Advent.

Saturday: A Real Advent

All members of the Sunday school class tried to make some decisions about our holiday party. Where should it be? What day? Should we have dinner or simply hors d'oeuvres? Possibly at the church this year? Or someone's home? Should we observe the rituals of the past or is this a time for alternatives?

Questions flooded the room. Hands flew up and down. Feelings were expressed. Laughter sounded through eager talk. Soon an invitation came. The date was settled. We jotted another date on our calendars. Because I enjoy this group and appreciate that for which they stand, I found myself anticipating the evening.

As I walked down the steps, I experienced that annual feeling of seasonal protocol. After all, there are cards to be sent and received, a gift list to balance, parties to arrange, homecomings and home-goings to anticipate, worship services to plan, the tree to trim, and traditions to uphold.

To settle for only this kind of Advent and Christmas is like settling for black and white when one could have "living color." Given the state of the world these days, not to mention the malnutrition of the inner person, we cannot afford such an Advent.

I want a season that helps me as a believer to experience the love and hope that is represented by the Incarnation. I want a real Advent this year!

Chapter Two

Second Week in Advent

In those days came John the Baptist, preaching in the wilderness of Judea, "Repent, for the kingdom of heaven is at hand." For this is he who was spoken of by the prophet Isaiah when he said, "The voice of one crying in the wilderness: Prepare the way of the Lord, make his paths straight." Now John wore a garment of camel's hair, and a leather girdle around his waist; and his food was locusts and wild honey. Then went out to him Jerusalem and all Judea and all the region about the Jordan, and they were baptized by him in the river Jordan, confessing their sins.

But when he saw many of the Pharisees and Sadducees coming for baptism, he said to them, "You brood of vipers! Who warned you to flee from the wrath to come? Bear fruit that befits repentance, and do not presume to say to yourselves, 'We have Abraham as our father'; for I tell you, God is able from these stones to raise up children to Abraham. Even now the axe is laid to the root of the trees; every tree therefore that does not bear good fruit is cut down and thrown into the fire.

"I baptize you with water for repentance, but he who is coming after me is mightier than I, whose sandals I am not worthy to carry; he will baptize you with the Holy Spirit and with fire. His winnowing fork is in his hand."

—Matthew 3:1–12

Steve Takatsuno

Sunday: Repentance as Preparation

The glory and strangeness of Christmas point in a side-door way to the mess we are in. Indirectly, this season whispers to us about the "out of focus world" in which we live.

It is not easy to explain the mess we are in. Many have tried. Few, if any, have succeeded. In his book, *The Coming Faith*, Carlyle Marney suggests that humankind "is the most savage of the beasts" —that our bite is poisonous, our hands are clubs, our feet are weapons. According to Marney, "nothing in nature is so well equipped for hating or hurting" as we are. Confuse us, and we lash out at anything. Crowd us, and we kill, rob, destroy. Deprive us and we retaliate. Impoverish us, and we burn villas in the night. Enslave us, and we revolt. Pamper us, and we may poison you. Hire us, and we may hate both you and the work. Love us too possessively, and we are never weaned. Deny us too early, and we never learn to love. Put us in cities, and all our animal nature comes out with perversions of every good thing. Mr. Marney clearly has a pessimistic view of human nature.

Marney, it seems to me, is partially correct, but there is also great good in humankind. Our bite is also sometimes sweet; our hands can also offer a caring touch; our feet may be helpers. Nothing in nature is so well equipped for loving and healing as we are. Confuse us and we often run for community; crowd us and we usually seek solutions. Deprive us, and we organize for a better tomorrow. Impoverish us, and we bargain collectively. Enslave us, and many of us will practice nonviolence. Pamper us, and we may instead seek strength. Hire us, and we usually work hard. Love us, and we are fulfilled. Deny us, and we seek. Put us in cities, and we try to enjoy life.

Society is a great composite picture of our power to harm. Society is also a great composite picture of our ability to do good. Art, culture, philosophy, order, and religion have all been used to tame the tiger within us. They have been used as expressions of the common good. We have tried many ways to tame the beast and express the good: the Ten Commandments of Moses, the great code of Hammurabi, Assyrian codes, Egyptian codes, Hindu laws, Oriental Yin-Yang, the corpus of Roman law, Stoic philosophy, the Greek notion of people—all these were attempts to tame the savagery within or to make a statement about what is meet and right. As noble as these thoughts were, none of these civilizers civilized.

Something more is needed if we are to come out of the wilderness we are in. That something more is spoken of by John the Baptist.

John the Baptist was not ostentatious or pretentious. Like Elijah who had gone before him, John wore a robe made of camel's hair with a leather belt knotted about his waist. The staples of his diet consisted of sweet, wild honey and locusts. He lived simply.

John chose not to live like the vast majority of Jews in his day. They were, by virtue of their occupations or voluntarily, entangled in the web of impurity which was woven into the fabric of political, economic, and social life under the Roman occupation. Those conditions and his own convictions led

John to the wilderness of Judea which was both a center of hope and a place of political refuge. It was in that same wilderness that God had tabernacled with his people for forty years before bringing them into the promised land. John had learned from his priestly father and from his Essenian background and his study of scripture that it was•in the wilderness that the way of the Lord was to be made straight. Many believed that the Messiah would first appear there.

It is entirely possible that John had united with a disciplined religious community which was living in the heart of the wilderness. They believed that they were preparing the way for the Lord's coming through the study of the law and strict obedience to all of the teachings which had been revealed to the prophets. This community saw itself as a "holy of holies" where sacrifice, obedience, and repentance served as atonements for sin. These people worked with great effort to be obedient to the law until the coming of the Messiah.

It was this kind of community which produced the preaching of John the Baptist. His preaching caught the attention of the masses. Persons eager to hear a new word came from Jerusalem, all Judea, and the vast territory around the Jordan. He was a man with a message, and the multitudes came to listen. Even in a confused and bewildering time like ours, people will come, and often at great inconvenience, if there is a message that heals people and sets them free.

John's message was directed to people who believed that the kingdom could be inherited. The emphasis in Jewish theology at that point in time was not so much on repentance as on acceptance of religious heritage. The typical Jew believed that one prepared for the Messiah by fastidiously and legalistically keeping the many rules and regulations of handed-down religion. John's teaching differed sharply with that understanding. He taught that one should prepare for the Messiah's coming with repentance and baptism. There seems no question that John took over the practice of baptism, including the emphasis on repentance, from the Essene sect but gave it a far more profound meaning. In later Christian thought baptism incorporated a man or woman into the covenant people of the Messiah, conceived as one with Israel of the Old Covenant. At the same time it was a token of repentance and an instrument of pardon.

John's constituency was remarkably like the modern Christian community where there is a deeply entrenched belief in religion by birthright. Large numbers of people feel very comfortable because they have been born into a congregation. They have grown up with the symbols, liturgy, legends, theology, and practices of the local church. Though there is a great value in religion that is nurtured, it is often void of confession and repentance.

I took Matthew's account of John the Baptist to an adult church school class in our congregation. After giving some background information and interpretation, I asked the class to give me some help in preparing a sermon on the theme of repentance. I said, "If you were in my place what would you say to this church about repentance?" Blank, sheepish stares lined their faces. One person said, "We are like the people of John's day. We are so close to it that we cannot hear the message." Another said, "It is like preaching to the choir. No one listens because we have been conditioned to hear something else." Yet another said, "Repentance is something we do in the corporate prayer not something we do in our hearts."

John the Baptist believed that the way out of the mess we are in is the way of repentance, because the "Kingdom of Heaven is at hand" (Mark 1:4). John preached that the Messiah could not be experienced until people had first repented of their sin. This Advent offers us the opportunity to repent as a way of preparing for the Messiah's birth. Other preparations will miss the mark, and alternative approaches will be off target, if we do not first repent our sins.

Repentance in the biblical sense is more than a change of mind or the feeling of regret or remorse. It is a decisive turning away from sin and back to God. The emphasis may rest on the negative side of turning away from sin, disobedience, or rebellion. It may also fall on the positive side, the turning back to God with the beginning of a new religious or moral life. That's what was new in John's preaching. He did not tell his eager listeners to be at ease in Zion. Nor did he advise them to be content with an inherited faith. He proclaimed loudly and forthrightly that his audience should prepare for the coming Messiah by repenting of sin. What was true then is true now. The way for us to prepare for a whispering Christmas is once again by way of repentance. Repentance has the mysterious effect of freeing us from our hurts, unfulfilled hopes, broken relationships, and moral failures.

Dr. Leslie Weatherhead once told a story about a man who needed to make a confession about a broken relationship between him and his wife. The man was an untiring factory worker who was burdened with heavy manual labor from early morning until late evening. His wife was a constant nag. She complained about the town, the nature of her husband's work, his low salary, and all of the things they did not have. As time passed the worker developed headaches, ulcers, and loss of weight. Out of respect and loyalty to his wife, he kept things tightly inside. Outwardly all seemed to be fine, but inwardly he was a "basket case."

After worship one Sunday, he requested an appointment with his pastor, Dr. Weatherhead. During the conference the man talked out his problems and repented for not being open and honest with his employer and his wife. He turned to God for the faith and strength that he needed for facing life. As time passed his headaches subsided, his ulcers got better, and his weight stabilized. When he confessed his hurt to another human being and to God, doors and windows were opened and he found new ways to cope with his problems. Repentance does not solve all of our problems, but it does have a strange way of setting us free. Dr. Jack Northrup, a pastoral counselor, says that just talking honestly about life often helps. He is correct.

I had a neighbor who was shy and very difficult to know. We would often wave and sometimes chat with one another over the back fence. As I came to know her better, I felt that something troubling was circulating deep within her inner being. As time passed, trust built a bridge between us. While leaning on the fence late one crisp November afternoon she said, "I have not shared this with many people. My daughter and I are alienated from one another, and I have not seen her for many years." She told me that her daughter had been married and divorced three times and that she had just received a telegram coldly stating that her daughter was about to be married for the fourth time. She said that they only communicated with telegrams and then only when there was a change of address or phone number.

This almost-retired school teacher spoke with feeling about how much she needed and wanted that daughter. She rehearsed what had gone wrong, the mistakes she had made, and how they had become like two ships passing in the night. After listening through several "fence conferences," I suggested that she might purchase a wedding gift and forward it with just the words "Love, Mother" inscribed on the card. With understandable hesitation, she did as I suggested. A few days later she came to my house with an oversized smile wrapped around her narrow face. "Joe," she said, "I just heard from my daughter. It's the first time she has called me in many years. She appreciated my gift and my note, and she is coming home for Christmas with her new husband."

During the visit there were many opportunities for leisurely conversation and reflection. Both mother and daughter did some confessing. My neighbor owned the error of her ways. Her "only child" daughter confessed her shortcomings. If that mother had never shared the ache inside her with another human being, she might have gone to her grave estranged from her only child. It was repentance which had the power to open the door to a restored relationship.

Sound and agonizing repentance is based on the belief that we do not stand alone against the elemental powers of this world. Whenever I repent of my sin before God and another person, I am saying that I do not stand alone against those forces that are about to overcome me. I am saying that I must be open and vulnerable and acknowledge my weakness before strength can come.

The mystery of repentance is that it tears down the walls that are between all of God's children. In late November of 1983 Americans watched "The Day After," a grim television depiction of a nuclear holocaust. There must be, according to the preaching of John the Baptist, a day before the day after. The day before must be a day of radical repentance when both Russia and the United States repent for having built the walls of nuclear weapons. Without repentance on both sides, the walls will grow taller and thicker. The issue is not who can drop the first bomb, but who can bring both sides to repentance.

Repentance takes the power out of the forces which carry the threat of destruction. If that is true with great social questions, it is also true with individuals. To say honestly, "I am an alcoholic," or "I cheat," or "I have wronged you," or "I have exploited you," or "my name is racist," or "I am tired of caring" is to take the strength out of the muscle which threatens to undo us. That's how we begin to get out of the mess we are in.

John the Baptist did not call for a superficial "I am sorry" kind of repentance. Nor did he ask us to work hard at doing better. He called for a kind of repentance where the "axe is laid to the root of the trees" (Matt. 3:10). Possibly John had drawn that thought from the prophet Isaiah who said:

> Behold, the Lord, the Lord of hosts
>   will lop the boughs with terrifying power;
> the great in height will be hewn down
>   and the lofty will be brought low.
> He will cut down the thickets of the forest
>   with an axe
> And Lebanon with its majestic trees will fall.
> —Isaiah 10:33–34

At this time before Christmas, it is important for us to hear what John and Isaiah were yearning to tell us. They were saying that a pruning is often necessary before there can be a bearing of fruit.. Without pruning there can be no fruit that befits repentance.

In the verses that follow Isaiah's lamentation on how the Lord will use the axe to cut the boughs, the great bushes, the thickets, and the majestic trees, he says:

> There shall come forth a shoot
>   from the stump of Jesse,
> and a branch shall grow out of his roots.
>   And the Spirit of the Lord shall rest upon him,
> the spirit of wisdom and understanding,
> the spirit of counsel and might,
> the spirit of knowledge and the fear
>   of the Lord.
> And his delight shall be in the fear
>   of the Lord.
>
> —Isaiah 11:1–3

Not until the tree is cut back to a stump can the new shoot spring forth. Without the pruning there is not the possibility of new life.

A few years ago my wife and I had the opportunity to attend a worship service in Shepherd's Field. It was about six weeks before Christmas when my thoughts were just beginning to turn toward Advent. A dry cold wind blew across the field that night. Stars were magnificently sprinkled across the blackened sky. Worshippers from all over the world had gathered there as a part of a worldwide convocation on evangelism. As we stood in the very field where tradition says that the shepherds attended their flocks by night, we could see the twinkle of lights from the city of Bethlehem. Feelings of warmth and contrition quietly moved through my inner being as I reflected upon the announcement of Christ's birth to those shepherds so many years ago.

As I worshipped in Shepherd's Field that night, I did not feel the need to tell God about my virtues, to list my accomplishments, to pat myself on the back, or to say, "Look at me, God, I am a fruit-bearing person." Quite the contrary. As I felt a vision of something more and something better, I was moved to a spirit of humility.

I wanted God to prune me. I wanted the broken limbs, the dead branches, the diseased bark cut out of my life. I wanted the bushy, thick places trimmed so that the light of God's love could shine in.

I am certain that we will not experience the joy of Christmas this year unless we first have a season of repentance. Without the pruning there cannot be new growth.

Daily Reflections

Monday: For Those Who Strike Out

I am the kid who never made the team. Every spring I would try out for the local baseball team, and every spring I would miss the cut. The fact is that I struck out so many times in tryouts that I no longer wanted to get up to bat. Life for some people is precisely that way. It is possible to strike out so often in life that one no longer has the will to get up to bat.

Newspapers often carry stories about God's poor who live on skid row, in box cars, at the mission, and on the streets of our cities. Many suggestions are made. Move the mission. Send them to a farm. Put them in a colony away from the city. After all, everyone wants to live in the country—don't they? Build a bigger jail. Close the liquor stores so the drunks cannot buy cheap wine. Warehouse them. Punish them. Convert them. Preach to them. Pray for them. The problem is not that we do not want to help. It is that we often do not know how.

Even if we do not know how to help, we can at least change our perceptions. Here we have a subculture of people who have lost the power to say "no." Don't be too judgmental, because many of us have lost the power to say "no" to desserts, booze, pills, discipline, etc. Our inability to say "no" should put us in touch with those who are more acquainted with degradation than with mercy.

I am sure the drunks were in downtowns long

before the mission or the Salvation Army. And I believe that Christ was there before any of them. I am not certain how to help, but I am certain that the Christ born in Bethlehem is with every derelict on every street corner, in every soup line, on every box car, in every flea-bitten hotel, in every gutter, in every city, in every square inch of the entire world.

People who have troubles remind us that life for any of us can be fragile and tenuous. They also remind us that God came in Christ both for those who can and those who cannot get up to bat one more time.

Tuesday: The Supporting Cast

The preacher, wanting to be alert to both the liturgical season and the needs of people, is forever pushed to select the appropriate topic for the Sunday sermon. If that is true throughout the year, it is dramatically important for Advent and Christmastide. The season is made rich and glorious by the message, the stories, the characters, and the biblical symbolism that fill the imagination.

For twenty years I have preached the themes of Advent. And for twenty years I have shared those themes through the center-stage people of the infancy narratives—Joseph, the wise men, the shepherds, the angel, the innkeeper, and all the rest. For twenty years I have neglected the "supporting cast" of persons like Elizabeth, Mary, and Anna. It is important to hear a word from God through these often overlooked people who surround the birth narratives.

After all, the play forever depends on the supporting cast. A drama cannot be produced without the stagehands and bit parts. As Advent begins to unfold, I am aware of the Elizabeths, Marys, and Annas that are still participating in the reenactment of the birth narrative.

God does not limit revelation to the superstars. But then God has always come to us in strange ways and in strange people: Moses, the murderer; Amos, the clown from the hills of Tekoa; John the Baptist in his strange leather getup, eating locusts and wild honey out in the desert; and of course Jesus, the stranger from Nazareth. God made his announcement not through the wife of Caesar Augustus but through the wife of a local carpenter.

Wednesday: It's Strange

The oversized billboard-type sign was perched outside the Sonic Burger restaurant in a West Tennessee county seat town. I had to blink twice before the message on the lighted sign registered in my brain. But there it was—big as a sunny day—and no one could deny what the two words said. Yep, sure enough. "Fried Pickles" were being prepared and sold in that establishment. Yes, I said "Fried Pickles!" According to my way of thinking that's strange, real strange, awesome strange. It would seem that a roadside place could advertise regular things like hamburgers, fries, hotdogs, milk shakes, and Cokes and do more business than with "Fried Pickles."

But there are a lot of things in this world almost as strange as fried pickles. Housing juveniles in jails designed for adults is strange. Trying to find peace by building MX missiles is strange. People of different races not being able to live in harmony is strange. Empty stomachs in a world of plenty is strange. Preachers of the gospel practicing more diplomacy than truth-telling is strange. Children without someone to love them is strange. Our stubborn refusal to reach out to one who is hurting is strange. Not saying "I love you" to a mate, child, or friend is strange. Serving our little gods is strange. Saying things we do not believe, living by half-truths, pretending that life is something other than what it is, and not being able to face life is strange. Not living while we are alive is strange. Trying to fit God into our notions of how God should and should not act is strange!

Actually, fried pickles don't seem so strange after all.

Thursday: From Activity to Meaning

I recently participated in a very significant event with the religious community of the city. As the event approached, I found myself filled with more and more anticipation. My anticipation pushed me to read, reflect, and puzzle. As a matter of fact, I got downright excited about that which was to come. The event happened. I participated. Unfortunately, I was left unaffected by the experience. The reason that I was untouched may have been within me, within the event, or a combination of both.

Likewise I puzzle over the possibility that we will pass through Advent but not experience a new "coming" of Christ's spirit in our midst. Yet Advent offers us the opportunity to reflect on the meaning of life from the vantage point of Christ's coming. As members of congregations we will reflect on his coming with pageantry, symbols, music, crafts, drama, proclamation, holy communion, study, fellowship, and service. Hopefully the activities of this season will add to the meaning of the season.

Passing through this season without being touched by it would make us like Rip Van Winkle who awakened not knowing that a revolution had taken place.

Open yourself to the coming of Christ and you will not approach Christmas unaffected.

Friday: Appreciating Others

The applause was thunderous, and one could hear voices calling "Dance!" "Dance!" "Sing!" "Sing!" Bow after bow was taken. Upon seeing that the audience would not relent, Yul Brynner motioned for the crowd to hush. A pin-drop silence fell over the massive Andrew Jackson Hall. The audience waited in silent anticipation and with great eagerness to hear what the actor wanted to say. With a soft, almost inaudible voice, Brynner spoke. "Some years ago Gertrude Lawrence, the great actress, died. She loved the stage and she loved applause. It was Gertrude Lawrence who really made 'The King and I' what it is today. Instead of the traditional minute of silence, let us have a minute of applause for this great actress." The misty-eyed audience responded with warm applause of appreciation as the great actor slipped silently behind the falling velvet curtain.

As we left our seats, the usher said, "You all got an extra tonight. That's the first time he has spoken to the audience. He's awesome, isn't he?"

Yes, sir, Mr. Usher, he is indeed "awesome." He is awesome not only because of his talent, but because he is gracious enough to give the credit to one who has gone before him.

On that night Yul Brynner was "king" because he took the position of quiet humility deferring to one who was greater. Like the cast in "The King and I," we all stand upon the shoulders of those who have gone before us. We are not self-made. We are in the debt of others. In most cases it is other people who have made us who we are.

Name your "Gertrude Lawrence." Applaud her. Take a bow to her. Thank God for her. More than that, strive to be a "Gertrude Lawrence" for someone, somewhere, sometime.

In this time prior to Christmas when our thoughts are beginning to turn to others, it would be entirely appropriate to put your benefactors on center stage before the audience of your heart.

Saturday: Differences Transcended

He stood alone on the tee box. He was tall, muscular, bearded, and somewhat awkward. "Bud," I said, "is he playing solo?" Bud nodded and then invited the stranger to play the next nine holes of golf with us. As we played, I learned he was from Ohio and was going to graduate school on the GI Bill. So friendly was this chap that I decided to tease him.

After about five holes I said, "If you stay in Nashville long enough, we'll teach you to eat black-eyed peas, grits, cornbread, and catfish." "I like German food," he responded with some emphasis on German. So abrupt was his retort that I carefully put the dietary habits of Southerners on the back burner. As he walked the fairway to the last green, he coasted over to me and asked in a church whisper, "Do you really eat catfish?" I nodded in the affirmative. "Really?" Again I motioned in the positive, growing curious at his insistence. "How could you?" he exclaimed. "Back home we throw them back or feed them to the cats."

Our regional food preferences are but one small indication of the differences that exist among people. We are not different altogether by choice but because our backgrounds and cultures have molded us to see life differently, hold various views, cling to divergent political philosophies, practice certain customs, and even to accept different images of God. We notice our differences in the global village, throughout our neighborhood, and around our family dinner table. We can no longer afford to run from these differences, fight them, or ignore them. They need to be understood so that we can be in touch with one another.

Advent proclaims that God came in Christ to transcend our differences and, thereby, to make us one. Christ came not to make us carbon copies of one another, but to bring us compassionately together.

Chapter Three **Third Week in Advent**

Now when John heard in prison about the deeds of the Christ, he sent word by his disciples and said to him, "Are you he who is come, or shall we look for another?" And Jesus answered them, "Go and tell John what you hear and see: the blind receive their sight and the lame walk, lepers are cleansed and the deaf hear, and the dead are raised up, and the poor have good news preached to them. And blessed is he who takes no offense at me."

As they went away, Jesus began to speak to the crowds concerning John: "What did you go out into the wilderness to behold? A reed shaken by the wind? Why then did you go out? To see a man clothed in soft raiment? Behold, those who wear soft raiment are in kings' houses. Why then did you go out? To see a prophet? Yes, I tell you, and more than a prophet. This is he of whom it is written, 'Behold, I send my messenger before thy face, who shall prepare thy way before thee.' Truly, I say to you, among those born of women there has risen no one greater than John the Baptist; yet he who is least in the kingdom of heaven is greater than he."

—Matthew 11:2–11

Sunday: Does Hope Abound?

That childhood Christmas is still not difficult to remember. I mark it by the gift of a Louisville Slugger, the finest baseball bat a boy could own. I could not have been prouder. It was clearly the most envied "stick," as we called it, in our neighborhood. "Son," my father said, "you must learn to hit with the label up or you will crack the bat." Life is that way. If we try to live without hope, living becomes like a bat with the label turned the wrong way. It runs the risk of cracking.

John the Baptist had every reason not to be hopeful. From his strict Essenian background, he had become one of the most popular preachers of his day. He had called the masses to repentance as a way of preparing for the coming Messiah. Jesus said that he was more than a prophet, meaning that he was a messenger who had been called of God to prepare for the coming of the "day of the Lord." So significant was he that Jesus went to him for baptism which was God's way of showing that the Messiah must be completely identified with his people, however different from sinners the Messiah must be.

John had also been a courageous preacher. He had labeled the Pharisees and Sadducees, the most outwardly religious people of his day, a "breed of vipers" because their faith was not fruit bearing. He accused them of wanting to be content with an inherited faith. Just because they were the children of Abraham did not give them an automatic place in the kingdom of God.

57

The Baptist was not given a place of honor for his unique contribution to the thought of his day. The authorities and religious leaders did not hear him. No wine was toasted in his honor. No applause thundered from the seats of the wise and powerful. John was thrown in prison for his effort to proclaim the coming kingdom of heaven. While in prison, with his dreams dashed and unfulfilled, John did not feel that hope abounded.

We can easily identify with this itinerant preacher, because we also feel the hopelessness of our generation. Paul, in his letter to the Romans, might have believed that hope should abound, but I am not quite so certain. "Abounding in hope" might be too strong a phrase for times like these. Almost every issue of the morning newspaper rehearses the many dreary problems that we face in the world today. Blacks still do not have their justice. Inflation has lessened, but unemployment has increased. War drags on and on in many countries. The population keeps exploding, bringing us ever so close to the horrors that we will face a generation from now if it is not drastically controlled. Many believe that polluted air has caused unpredictable weather patterns. Our cities are strangling to death with traffic and urban rot. The number of young people involved in the drug culture continues to move upward like an escalator. Hunger stalks the planet. The walls between people grow higher and thicker as nuclear weapons are built and planted at strategic locations around the globe. Tensions between the generations and within the generations tighten. The list could be expanded.

The point is that it is difficult to have hope in a world like this. We may not be in a Roman jail like John the Baptist, but we certainly feel trapped by the whole dreary bit. However it is our world—our responsibility—and we had better not forget it. Instead we must try at this season of Advent to hear a word of hope.

Remember the shopping season which produced a hunger for a little plaything called the Cabbage Patch doll? Many merchants ran out of their supply well before Thanksgiving. People stood in long, twisting lines clutching two tens and a five hoping to purchase one of those flat-faced, diaper-wearing dolls. As the supply shortened, the demand increased. The need to secure one for a child's Christmas stocking spread like a fever across the land. One man flew all the way to London, England, to purchase three of them for his children. A grandfather was trampled while waiting in a chain store line. Two women got in a fight. Children cried and pleaded for the privilege of owning a Cabbage Patch doll.

Twelve women, upon hearing a fake radio announcement, went to a football field hoping that an airplane would drop some dolls into their waiting hands. They were, of course, disappointed. Their hopes were unrealistic and, in this case, even foolish.

Whereas it is important for us to be skeptical of pale hopes, it is also essential that we do not hope for too much. The early church made that mistake. Early Christians believed that Christ was going to come immediately and with great fanfare. But now almost two thousand years have passed and Christ has not come as the early church expected. The early church clearly painted itself into a corner by hoping for too much.

We will be far better off if we can keep our hopes realistic. My father was sick and confined to our home for a number of weeks before his death. The sheer monotony of being homebound was broken by frequent visits by his pastor. Being a committed coffee drinker, my father would pour his pastor cup after cup of coffee. Week after week, the pastor came to empathize with, listen to, and shepherd my father. My dad's pastor never hoped for too much. He never believed that my father would get well, but he did hope that by his presence my father would be able to cope with his illness and handle his coming death well. After my father's funeral, I learned that this devoted pastor abhorred coffee. And yet by his coming, he had the hope that my father could handle the limitations of his life much better. That, in my judgment, was a realistic hope.

It is important that we not hope for too much nor too little, but it is even more important that we keep hoping. There is a section of our city that was once a wonderful-place-to-live kind of neighborhood. Pride in the neighborhood was evidenced by the manicured lawns, well-painted houses, and the orderly flow of people. A few years ago the word came that an expressway was going to be constructed right through the center of that portion of town. When the residents learned this rather disquieting news, some of them ceased painting their buildings, repairing their roofs, and taking care of their gutters. When those people lost hope in the future, they ceased tending to the present. Without hope we cannot be pulled into a new future and a new way of life.

Strange as it seems, Christian hope is often found in unlikely places. In fact, Christian hope has a way of burning brightest on the most darkened stage. Christmas itself is not observed in the beautiful springtime. It is a celebration at the dark winter solstice. The significance of the date does not have historical importance. In *Proclamation 2*, Frederick Borsch and David Napier say the significance is, instead, theological.

There is no evidence of any kind regarding the date of Jesus' birth. His nativity began to be celebrated on December 25 in Rome during the early part of the fourth century (A.D. 336) as a Christian counterpart to the pagan festival, popular among the worshipers of Mithras, called Sol Invictis, the Unconquerable Sun. At the very moment when the days are the shortest and darkness seems to have conquered light, the sun passes its nadir. Days grow longer, and although the cold will only increase for quite a long time, the ultimate conquest of winter is sure. This astronomical process is a parable of the career of the Incarnate One. At the moment when history is blackest, and in the least expected and obvious place, the Son of God is born. And although his life proceeds from a manger to a cross, and his conflicts only increase, the ultimate conquest of death is sure.

Edmund A. Steimle held to that same position in *From Death to Birth:*

It is in the dark moments of their history that the ancient prophets and writers—and Christians after them—have talked most eloquently about hope. Because they knew that hope has to be held close to all that seems to deny it if it is to mean anything. Anyone can hope when things go well. But when things look bleak and dark, then the God of hope can offer us something.

It was at a dark moment in John's history when he sent some of his friends to ask Jesus the question: "Are you he who is to come, or shall we look for another?" (Matt. 11:3). That kind of question, raised by a man in prison, emerges out of the hope that possibly Jesus of Nazareth is the Messiah. John raised the question as if he wanted to make certain that his life and preaching had not been in vain.

Or possibly John sent that probing question to Jesus because he was confused. He had reason to be mixed up about who Jesus really was. Had John not baptized Jesus? Had he not seen the dove? Had not both Jesus and John turned backflips in their mothers' wombs at about the same time? Had John not listened to the sermons and seen the miracles of Jesus?

It is just possible that even John was not absolutely certain that Jesus was the authentic Messiah because he did not fulfill many of the expectations of that day. Many of John's contemporaries believed that the Messiah would come as royalty, but Jesus came in manger rags. Others felt that the Messiah would come from kings, but Jesus was born as the son of a hardworking carpenter. In the eyes of many he had the wrong lineage. The average person in the street believed that the Messiah would have the strength of military power, but Jesus possessed the strength of humility. His characteristics of vulnerability, love, and service seemed contrary to the common expectation of Messiah.

Therefore John, suffering from a loss of hope and confusion, sent his disciples to Jesus with the question: "Are you he who is to come, or shall we look for another?" (Matt. 11:3).

Like John the Baptist, we know a lot about Jesus, but we are also pulled by the promises of many messiahs who promise us hope if we will give them allegiance. Hedonism, "thingism," cultism, militarism, narcissism, and the selfish use of power have a subtle and convincing way of telling us, "We can deliver you from your hopelessness. We can meet the deepest longing of your life. We can feed the hunger and quiet the unsettled feeling within you."

At this time of the year when the messiahs of

commercialism are so well organized and when we are blinded by our busy and frenzied activity, it is easy for us to be confused about where we shall experience the Messiah.

The answer that Jesus gave to John's disciples should give us some hope at this Advent season. Jesus answered the friends of John by saying: "Go and tell John what you hear and see: the blind receive their sight and the lame walk, lepers are cleansed and the deaf hear, and the dead are raised up, and the poor have good news preached to them. And blessed is he who takes no offense at me" (Matt. 11:4–6). That answer may not have been completely satisfactory to John the Baptist and it may not altogether satisfy us. It seems to be a nonanswer. There is no confirmation or verification in it. Jesus did not boast about messiahship. Nor did he make strong claims about himself. Instead, he drew the attention of John's disciples to the new life that was being given because of his presence in the world. Life was being given to the blind, lame, lepers, deaf, dead, and the poor.

I have the strong feeling, as Christmas draws near, that hope does abound if we know where to look for it. If we look for it in the tired expectations created by a culture, we will probably be disappointed. If we look for it in the words of the powerful and prestigious, we will be saddened. If we look for hope in the rituals of the selfish and self-centered. our looking will be in vain.

Does hope abound? Yes, it abounds where love is flowing out on all living things. It abounds wherever and whenever life is being given.

I spoke during Advent at a nearby high-rise residence for the elderly. After my speech on "Where Does One Find the Messiah?" an old man started speaking in response: "I just rented my house and moved here a few months ago. My wife recently died after a long bout with cancer. My children are dear to me, but I do not see them very often. I am an old, cranky man now. Because of an illness over which I have no control, I am probably facing my last Christmas. As I look back over my life, I have learned one big lesson. The main lesson I have learned is that I can't love or be loved too much." There, right there, is where one experiences the coming Christ. It is forever in the midst of life-giving love that Christ is most real.

The second verse of the hymn, "Lead On, O King Eternal," is a magnificent statement about the abounding hope. Listen to it:

> Lead on, O King eternal,
>   Till sin's fierce war shall cease,
> And holiness shall whisper
>   The sweet amen of peace.
> For not with swords loud clashing,
>   Nor roll of stirring drums,
> With deeds of love and mercy,
>   The heavenly kingdom comes.

Daily Reflections

Monday: Holding On

She has been to and from the hospital, but her spirits are not whipped down by the illness after illness and surgery after surgery she has endured. She tells me that she has had too many winters and too many birthdays. Maybe so. Maybe not. How does one judge that? In addition to her many trips to health care services, life circumstances have forced her to move many times, with each transition taking her to smaller and smaller apartments. Each move has required her to dispose of more belongings. She has had to "strip down," "get lean," and lead a very simple lifestyle in order simply to live. Through it all she has maintained a quiet zest for life that would be envied by most of us who spend so much of our energy trying to hoard more things into bigger barns.

On a recent visit I inquired about her tenacious ability to cope. "How have you managed?" I said. "Well, for one thing," she said, "I have read my Bible and kept my curtains. No matter where I live I have the same book and I have the same old curtains." "I understand the Bible but why the curtains?" I replied. With a sly twinkle in her blue eyes, she said, "They both give me something to hold on to."

Likewise our religious and family rituals give us something to "hold on to." Christmas would be far less meaningful without Christmas Eve holy communion or without my wife's five-pound fudge. Both give me something to hold on to.

Tuesday: No House in the Room

Sean, a three-year-old member of our congregation, recently made an interesting comment about the Christmas story. He plainly said that Jesus was born in a stable because there was "no house in the room."

Sean, I would like to say to you that it is not so bad to have the details blurred and confused. Mature adults do that, too. Our lamentations contradict our Emmanuels. We are not certain if it is Bethlehem or Nazareth. The Annunciation spills over into the Magnificat. Did Augustus or Quirinius send out the decree? Were Joseph and Mary married or engaged? Was it the Lord or angels who made known the birth to the shepherds. We forget why Herod felt tricked by the Wise Men. In our minds Matthew's account and Luke's portrayal are meshed with one another. You see, Sean, there are not many "big people" who are readily capable of telling the story without botching the details or confusing the characters.

Someday, Sean, if you keep probing with your questions, you will come to understand that the message of the story is far more important than the particulars. In fact, you can neatly arrange all of the details and still miss the message of Christmas entirely.

I hope you will experience in the cradle of your heart that which the Gospel writers were straining to tell you with their word pictures. The message is that God's loving manifestation and reign is often brought about by God alone without the help of anyone. Christians represent one portion of God's family who respond to that display of God's love with faith.

Sean, the meaning of the message is as profound as the story is simple. We grown-ups try to live by it, although we do not fully understand it either. So tell the story your own way, Sean, and we will understand with our hearts.

Wednesday: Intrusions

The Wightman Chapel on the Scarritt College campus was jammed with believers who wanted to experience the drama, joy, and feelings that can uniquely come through a Festival of Lessons and Carols as presented by the Scarritt College Chapel Choir. Decor, anticipation, excitement, liturgy, bells, greenery, candles, and fanfare all contributed to the glorious event. Only those of us who work with such experiences know how much psychic and physical preparation goes into such a service. They do not begin at the appointed time. They originate weeks and months ahead of the specified date. They loom, press, float, dodge, and intervene into one's life pattern.

The worship service was interrupted not once but many times by the loud talking, crying, and squealing of a child. So vocal was the child that we found ourselves being forced to listen to the youngster while trying to experience the service. Unfortunately the child did not give us a choice. He forced us into a preoccupation with his antics. Parental courtesy was absent. Respect was not given.

As much as I wanted the child to be silent or taken out or at least moved to the back row of the balcony, I know that real life is not this way.

Advent and Christmas are always marked by intrusions. Many secular interruptions keep us from focusing in on the meaning of this season. Respect for that which is symbolized by Christmas is often absent.

We must live out our faith, worship, and witness in the midst of constant diversion and intrusion. It was not quiet in the manger!

Thursday: Present with the Poor

The successful and distinguished young man stood with self-confidence before an audience of over three hundred. "I am going to take my children," he said, "to help deliver boxes this Christmas. I want them to see what it is like out there." It was clear that he was going to make his once-a-year pilgrimage to the doorstep of a needy home.

It is easy to be judgmental about that level of caring, but we must be careful because many of us find convenient ways to help the poor. We serve on the boards of agencies, belong to organizations, give an offering to world hunger, drop a quarter in the Salvation Army kettle, pay our church pledge, give away our used clothing, tip the carolers who come to sing. We generally act like decent, middle-class people are supposed to behave about such matters. All the things that I have mentioned are extremely important because, like an army, the supply line must be kept strong. If the supply lines are not cared for, the battles cannot be fought in the trenches.

There is a need, however, which goes beyond giving help to the poor. That need is for us, as individual Christians, to reflect upon how we shall be present *with* the poor. The God who came in Jesus of Nazareth came as One clothed in humility and poverty. Could it be that this God leans toward the poor and expects Christ's people to do the same?

Friday: Weakness

We called him "Mac." He was over fifty, overweight, red-faced, verbose, always chomping on a cigar, a barber by trade, not well educated, and extremely interested in people who lived with his problem—alcoholism. Mac taught me a great deal, not only about alcoholism, but also about the life that flows like a quiet stream through people. Though he did not hold a Ph.D., he had the wisdom to let life educate him.

Mac taught me that the members of Alcoholics Anonymous have a two-sided solution to life's difficulties. They turn their problems over to God, but they also ask others for help. It's difficult enough for most of us to turn our problems over to God, but to ask somebody else for help—there's the rub. Mac and his friends at Alcoholics Anonymous taught me that our very weakness and our need to ask others for help inadvertently create authentic fellowship. The true church cannot exist where everyone is strong. It is, at its best, a mutual society of the weak helping the weak.

We have been conditioned to think of a great leader as one who can help the weak, but a more effective leader is one who knows the weak help the weak and find strength together. Everyone needs help sometime from someone.

In *New Seeds of Contemplation,* Thomas Merton, the notable Catholic monk, describes hell as being "where no one has anything in common with anybody else except the fact that they all hate one another and cannot get away from one another and from themselves."

Christmas, more than any time of the year, reminds us that God was revealed in the weakness and vulnerability of a tiny baby—not to rule over us but to dwell with us.

If God, Mac, and Thomas Merton are correct, then we need to carefully rethink how God comes to us.

Saturday: Peace

It happened in a symbolic way at the All-Church Picnic. The staff, after having trounced the Sanctuary Choir in volleyball on Saturday, was locked in a fierce battle with the Graham-Inquirers Class who had thrashed the Covenant Class to earn a place in the championship game. The game was close. The stakes were high. Both teams were playing for "bragging rights."

Just as the competition was reaching a fevered pitch, the game was interrupted by three-year-old Sarah Isbell. She tiptoed through a maze of players and edged over the boundary rope in an effort to bring her daddy a handpicked bouquet of wild weeds and flowers mixed with clover. The game stopped as her dad, with his uncommon patience, tended to the needs of Sarah by accepting her special gift. While the rest of us watched this tender display of affection, someone said, "That could stop a war." Indeed it could. A pretty little girl bringing flowers to the battlefield could make a far more loving statement than whatever it is that causes nations to go to war with each other.

If this suggestion seems abnormal, absurd, foolish, and amusing, it is no more ridiculous than the fabulous amount of money, planning, energy, anxiety, and care which go into the production of weapons which almost immediately become obsolete and have to be scrapped. It is no more ridiculous than the plans to annihilate not thousands, but millions of civilians and soldiers, men, women, and children without discrimination, while inevitably inviting the same annihilation for ourselves and our loved ones.

Nor is the suggestion any more ridiculous than believing that the teachings, lifestyle, and values of Jesus are the basis for a true and lasting peace. To say that he is the Prince of Peace is as simple, profound, and full of meaning as little Sarah bringing flowers to her father.

Chapter Four

Fourth Week in Advent

Now the birth of Jesus Christ took place in this way. When his mother Mary had been betrothed to Joseph, before they came together she was found to be with child of the Holy Spirit; and her husband Joseph, being a just man and unwilling to put her to shame, resolved to divorce her quietly. But as he considered this, behold, an angel of the Lord appeared to him in a dream, saying, "Joseph, son of David, do not fear to take Mary your wife, for that which is conceived in her is of the Holy Spirit; she will bear a son, and you shall call his name Jesus, for he will save his people from their sins." All this took place to fulfil what the Lord had spoken by the prophet: "Behold, a virgin shall conceive and bear a son, and his name shall be called Emmanuel" (which means, God with us). When Joseph woke from sleep, he did as the angel of the Lord commanded him; he took his wife, but knew her not until she had borne a son; and he called his name Jesus.

—Matthew 1:18–25

John Netherton

Sunday: Beyond the Expected

I have a habit of inviting lay people to work with me on scriptural passages from which I will be preaching on the following Sunday. I will do this with church school classes and various lay groups. Usually someone will read the passage and I will provide comments about the author, setting, and situation of the text. After initial observations I will ask the group such questions as: "What does this text say to you about life as you experience it?" "What does the author say to you about you?" "How would you argue or take issue with the text?" After we have discussed those problems and possibilities, I will ask: "If you were preaching to this congregation from this passage, what would you say?" Often the responses inform my thinking as I prepare to preach from a given portion of the Bible.

One December I took the text of Matthew 1:18–25 to a young adult church school class for the purpose of study, reflection, and response. My preconceived notions about how they would treat this passage of scripture were not at all on target. I thought they would be interested in Emmanuel or the virginity of Mary or why the angel said what was said. I fully anticipated a lengthy discussion about what it means to say that "God is with us." My hunches were wrong. The feelings of these young people were drawn to Joseph. They identified with the difficult situation in which Joseph found himself. Immediately, they sensed the difficult choice he had to make.

The choice between two goods is often more difficult than the choice between something intrinsically good and supremely bad. That, according to the Gospel of Matthew, is the kind of choice that Joseph, the foster father of Jesus, had to make. Joseph was in a bind. His betrothed was found to be pregnant before they became husband and wife.

The process of being married in those days consisted of two steps: a formal exchange of consent before witnesses (Mal. 2:14) and the subsequent taking of the bride to the groom's family home (Matt. 25:1–13). The consent or "betrothal" was usually entered into when the girl was between twelve and thirteen years of age. This would usually constitute a legal marriage in our usage, since it gave the young man rights over the girl. She was henceforth known as the man's wife and any infringement on his marital rights could be punished as adultery. Yet the wife continued to live at her own family home, usually for about a year.

After twelve months there was a formal transferral or taking of the bride to the husband's family home where he and his family assumed her support. In Galilee it was also understood that the wife had to be taken to her husband's home as a virgin. One can see in reading Matthew that Joseph and Mary were in the stage of matrimonial procedure between the two steps. It was precisely between those two steps that Mary "was found to be with child." Thus the stage was set for an agonizing human decision.

What should Joseph do? Should he leave Mary, thereby putting her to shame, or should he divorce her quietly? The law permitted him to do either. According to the law, if a woman was found guilty of premarital sexual intercourse, she was to be stoned to death at the door of her father's house. There is very little evidence that such a penalty was typically imposed at the time of the Gospel, but a public repudiation would certainly bring lasting shame upon the woman. Joseph would have been fulfilling his legal duty by charging Mary openly with infidelity and repudiating her. There is no doubt that both scripture and tradition placed the ball squarely in Joseph's court.

The information contained in scripture about Joseph can help us understand why he made the decision as he did. His name is recorded only a few times in the New Testament and then almost exclusively in the birth and childhood stories of Jesus. We know that he followed the trade of carpentry, and it is commonly thought that Jesus, as a young man, worked in Joseph's carpenter shop. In the Gospel of John, Jesus is referred to as simply the "Son of Joseph" which might have implied that Joseph was well known as an able and skilled craftsman.

According to Matthew, Joseph was a resident of the Galilean hill town of Bethlehem who later settled in Nazareth, possibly because of the horrible conditions in Judea under the unjust and tyrannical Archelaus. There he followed his trade and reared his family.

The scriptures open only a few windows for us to peer into the life and character of Joseph. He was with Mary by the manger, at the circumcision, and when the boy was presented at the Temple. Both he and Mary quietly marveled over the blessing of Simeon, the old priest (Luke 2:33–35). The reader can feel his anxiety over the search for Jesus who, as a boy of twelve, got lost in the city (Luke 2: 41–48). He is described as a just man by which is meant that he was a devout servant of God and regulated his life according to the standards of the law. One also notes a kind of gentle wisdom in his makeup.

Matthew pictures Joseph as frequently receiving guidance from angels in dreams: to flee into the land of Egypt because of the meanness of Herod, to return from Egypt after his death, and to settle in Galilee rather than Judea. The biblical snapshots of Joseph differ in their presentation, but they do paint Joseph as a man of genuine piety and genuine character.

In spite of all of his strengths, Joseph was afraid to take pregnant Mary to his father's house. God was asking him to make a decision when all of the data was not in. He clearly understood what it meant to be just and honorable in this situation, but God was asking him to go far beyond the legal requirements. He was being asked to assume responsibility for a pregnant teenager with only the voice of an angel as his encouragement. He was being called to make a faith response to a very difficult life situation.

Like Joseph, we are often called by the forces of life to make hard decisions when there is very little to go on. One spring I received a phone call from a district superintendent in another United Methodist annual conference wanting me to leave my home conference. He spoke for the bishop in saying that I was needed at a church in Nashville, Tennessee. I was unable to focus in on the important questions and issues because the phone call had come as such a complete surprise. A mixture of excitement and fear surged through me. If my wife and I said yes, our secure and safe little world would soon be upended. If we said no, we might miss a new and challenging opportunity for service. I was given little time to reflect on this important decision because the superintendent needed our answer by 9:00 a.m. the next morning.

I knew almost nothing about the congregation in Nashville. Though I had attended seminary only a few blocks from the church, I knew it only from the outside. I had washed clothes in a tiny laundromat directly across from the church building. While waiting for my clothes to wash, I would often muse about what went on in that church across the street. Who were these people and to what were they committed? What dreams did they dream and how visionary were their visions? Was it a status church or a servant church or a combination of both? Was the pulpit prophetic and compassionate? Were the people engaged in the struggles of the world? Was faith taken seriously or treated as a boundary matter? These were the questions I had casually asked myself as I listened to the "thump, thump" of the washing machines. Now, in the face of a difficult choice, the questions were no longer casual.

Like Joseph, I had to make my decision based on trust and not evidence. It had to be a faith and not a fact decision. It was a decision that I was being asked to make with very little information at my finger tips. Strange as it now seems, I felt led to Nashville, and I have felt led to stay.

The decisions of life do not often come easy and clear-cut. Neatness, clarity, and precision are not often their characteristics. Many of them are made without being fully able to count the cost. Choosing a mate, bearing children, deciding a vocation, electing to change careers, and building friendships are decisions that must be made while not knowing the future. When dealing with the rock hard decisions of life, we can make them based only upon what is lawful, just, and conventional, or we can let mercy inform what we decide.

There is the strong possibility that Joseph decided as he did because he had come to understand God as a God of mercy. In reading the Hebrew scriptures Joseph had learned that God's mercy was manifested in many different ways: in forgiveness, such as

God's deliverance of his chosen nation from their enemies; in the gathering of the exiled people and the restoration of them to their land; in God's provision for them in the wilderness; in restoration of the people to communion with God. Over and over God gave himself to his bride, Israel, not out of duty, but out of love.

The limits and demands of mercy were governed by a structure of communal relationships. The closest ties known by any Hebrew were those of family. Within the family circle, mercy was expected as a way of life. Where a family was, there was mercy. Mercy was first to be rendered in the family and then in the tribe or community. In Hebrew thought, a special claim to mercy was given to children, the poor, the aged, the fatherless, and the widows. Joseph was ingrained with an understanding of life which said that truly to love God was to love others. Mercy given to men and women was mercy given to God. Thus, the written law was clear about what was permitted in a given situation and tradition was unambiguous about the importance of mercy.

At no other season of the year do so many practice mercy. Even the questions that we raise during the other eleven months do not surface during Advent and Christmas. From January until the first of December we ask questions like: "Are they really hungry?" "Is there a real need in that family?" "Do they really deserve it?" Or we make statements like: "If they would just work hard, they could support themselves." "All we owe people is an opportunity." "Let's help those who help themselves." "Let's give to those who deserve it."

Those of us who are followers of Jesus experience uneasy feelings when we make such statements, because we know that Jesus responded to human need with compassion. When the New Testament describes Jesus' reaction to human need, it uses a verb which means "to be moved in one's bowels." The Hebrews regarded the bowels as the seat of human emotion especially of tenderness, benevolence, and pity. The bowels were for the Hebrews, equivalent to the heart for us, as the seat of compassion. When Jesus was touched by raw, human need, the New Testament says that he was moved in his bowels with pity, compassion, and mercy. Also, such feelings in Jesus gave rise to acts of mercy. His compassion led him to heal the blind, to cleanse the leper, to teach the ignorant, to raise the dead, and to feed the hungry. If we listen to the spirit of Christ during this "Winter Lent," there is the possibility that we will be moved by his living presence to that which mercy requires.

In addition to those tangible things we give at this season of sharing, there is something more that needs to be given. If we want to give a very important gift this year, we will give ourselves to a life whose roots are planted in the soil of mercy.

On a crisp Thanksgiving Sunday evening I offered the worst sermon that I had preached in six months. In the sermon I said, "We are gathered here this morning" while it was pitch black outside. I referred to the live flowers in the sanctuary when they were artificial. I forgot an important point because I was not properly prepared. No one had to convince me that my preaching was a long way from the best that I could offer. Following the service, my youngest daughter, who almost never compliments a sermon, gave me a kiss and said, "Good job, Dad." I did not deserve that praise, but in giving it she went beyond the expected and practiced mercy toward me. When I felt her mercy, my spirits were restored. In going beyond the ordinary, my daughter was Joseph to me.

Like the world in which Joseph and Mary lived,

our generation does not deserve the Messiah. We are not good enough, wise enough, or loving enough to deserve an experience of the Messiah's birth. Thankfully, Advent is a time when we remember that God does not give the world what it deserves. He gives the world what it needs: One who "will save his people from their sins" (Matt 1:21).

After the church school class had talked about Joseph for almost an hour, a young woman said, "The real question for me is whether I could have accepted the baby as the son of God." Her question went straight to the heart of the matter because, like Joseph, we have to decide if we will act mercifully, which will make possible a new experience of Christ's birth in our day. As with Joseph, that decision rests squarely upon our shoulders. We do not deserve the gift of this Child, and yet we are once again given the opportunity to receive him.

Our decision is far-reaching. It is not like deciding whether or not to have another cup of coffee. There are those who want to make a decision to receive the Baby, but can't. And there are those who can receive the Baby, but will not. Then there are you and I and that decision becomes ours. The world anxiously waited for the decision that Joseph would make and the world now waits for our decision.

Chapter Five **Christmas Eve**

In those days a decree went out from Caesar Augustus that all the world should be enrolled. This was the first enrollment, when Quirinius was governor of Syria. And all went to be enrolled, each to his own city. And Joseph also went up from Galilee, from the city of Nazareth, to Judea, to the city of David, which is called Bethlehem, because he was of the house and lineage of David, to be enrolled with Mary his betrothed, who was with child. And while they were there, the time came for her to be delivered. And she gave birth to her first-born son and wrapped him in swaddling cloths, and laid him in a manger, because there was no place for them in the inn.

And in that region there were shepherds out in the field, keeping watch over their flock by night.

—Luke 2:1–8

John Netherton

Christmas Eve: Away with the Stable

If we could change some of our images about the Christmas story, it would mean more to us. If we could get the birth narrative straight, it would not be diminished, but enriched.

Luke records the incident of Christ's birth in a very simple and a very beautiful way: "[Mary] gave birth to her first-born son and wrapped him in swaddling cloths, and laid him in a manger, because there was no place for them in the inn."

Regardless of the stories that we have been told and hear about the little Bethlehem hotel being full, in spite of all of the criticism that we have heaped upon the innkeeper because he sent pregnant Mary outside to a cold stable, and no matter how many stables are erected in homes and on church parking lots, there is the possibility that Jesus was not born in a stable.

The Gospel of Luke does not mention Mary and Joseph arriving at Bethlehem at the last minute. Nor does Luke say that they scurried around to find a place to lodge because the baby was about to be born. Luke simply says "while they were there"—as if they had arrived several days ahead of Jesus' birth.

Luke makes no mention of a stable. He merely comments on the fact that Mary "gave birth to her first-born son and wrapped him in swaddling cloths and laid him in a manger." Luke wrote not one word about a hotel or an innkeeper who cold-heartedly turned the family away. There is no way to know how many Christmas pageants have portrayed the bad innkeeper who turned Mary and Joseph away from the door. According to Luke's Gospel that hard innkeeper and his tiny inn do not exist.

Luke tells the story another way.

The word in Luke which is typically translated "inn" is the Greek word *kataluma.* It is interesting to note that in the story of the Good Samaritan, Luke does not use the word *kataluma* to describe the inn to which the beaten man was taken. He uses another word to describe a place of lodging beside the Jericho Road. However, Luke tells about Jesus sending two of his disciples to find a *kataluma* for the serving of the Last Supper. Thus the word *kataluma* in Luke literally means a "guest room."

As Luke tells the story of the nativity, it is just possible that a proper translation would be something like this: "She gave birth to her first-born son and laid him in a manger because there was no place for them in the guest room" (AP).

Logic would suggest that there is some basis for this translation. Bethlehem probably had no inn or hotel since it was only six miles from Jerusalem, a mere two-hour walk. Furthermore, Bethlehem was not located on a main highway. The Roman roads in that region bypassed the City of David and went directly to Jerusalem. In all probability this small village had no need for an inn.

If Mary and Joseph had come there for a census, it is not unlikely that they had relatives living in Bethlehem with whom they stayed. It is possible that the carpenter from Nazareth and his young wife arrived a few days before the birth of their son and found the *kataluma,* the "guest room," already occupied by other relatives and guests. Since there was no room in the guest room, they may have lodged in the main room with the homeowner and his family. Thus, it may be that Jesus was not born in the inn or guest room but right out in the middle of the main room of the house.

We cannot fully appreciate the message of Luke unless we first understand the configuration of a Palestinian house. In those days a peasant's house was a simple, one-room affair. A man, his wife, their family, and all of their belongings were concentrated in one main room. If the owner of the house had sufficient resources, he would build a small room, adjacent to the main room, that was called an *inn* or *kataluma.* It was not uncommon for travellers to be offered a couple's guest room or inn as a place of lodging.

In the dead cold of winter it was not uncommon for a Palestinian family to bring into their house all of the livestock. This provided shelter for the animals and the heat of the beasts' bodies provided warmth for all who resided in the house. Usually the central room had an upper and a lower level. The family lived on the upper level while the cattle were kept on the lower level, possibly a foot or two lower than the rest of the house. On the step, next to where the cattle were lodged, there would have been a manger area. The location for the manger was a place scooped out to create a trough where the cattle could be fed. It was in that manger area, right in the middle of the house, that peasant Palestinian women gave birth to their children, so that the newborn might have the comfort of the manger's straw.

Listen carefully to what Luke is saying to his reader when he tells the story in this way. He is saying that Mary gave birth to Jesus right in the middle of the house because there was no room in the *kataluma* or guest room. Luke wanted his readers to hear something very special. He wanted his words to convey the notion that Jesus, the Son of God, was born, not off in the guest room, but right in the midst of smelly hay, snorting animals, anxious on-lookers, and in the tenderness and love of the family circle. Jesus, our saviour, was born just like all of the other children of that day. He was tenderly placed precisely where all other children of that day were cradled. When the magi arrived from afar, they came, as Matthew says, "into the house (where) they saw the child with Mary his mother" (Matt. 2:11).

If we experience the birth of Christ on this Christmas Eve, it will not be in the guest rooms of our lives, but right in the middle of it all. We will experience his birth right in the midst of people who love each other. We will feel his birth not in the *kataluma*, but in the pain of the world where his influence still says to "be reconciled to God" (2 Cor. 5:20). We will see his yearning to be born again in the Middle East where his voice still cries out for peace on earth and good will. We will find him tonight, not in the side rooms of life but with the poor, the imprisoned, and the hungry. If we listen closely we can still hear his voice saying, "As you did it to one of the least of these my brethren, you did it to me" (Matt. 25:40).

One of the traditions in my family is for us to gather at my wife's home on Christmas Day to break bread and open gifts. For almost twenty-three years I have joined with the family in that ritual. Until my wife's grandfather died, one of the tender moments of every December twenty-fifth was Granddaddy's prayer before the Christmas feast. All of the family would gather in one room and Granddaddy, his voice quiet but confident, would pray the same prayer every year. "Help us," he would say, "not to forget the birth of the One whom we remember on this day." He would pray that simple prayer right in the midst of it all: in the midst of the aroma of the almost-done turkey; in the midst of eager grandchildren; in the midst of a large room littered with wrapping paper; and in the midst of growling stomachs and tender taste buds. Granddaddy had never heard of the *kataluma*, but he prayed as if he had not pushed Christ into the guest room of his life.

Frederick Buechner, a well-known writer and preacher, was invited to teach a course in preaching at a Protestant seminary. Uncertainty gripped him because he had never ventured into teaching homiletics. In the beginning he taught his students how to draft introductions, conclusions, and thesis statements. Toward the middle of the semester he came to the silent conclusion that what he was teaching the students did not amount to very much. After apparent failure, he took a different approach. Instead of teaching a theory of preaching, he decided to teach his students about feelings. He said, "I tell them to pay special attention to those times when they find tears in their eyes."

That's where Christ is born. If we want Christ to be born in the cradles of our hearts tonight, we might do well to look for him in those experiences which cause the emotions to surface in our eyes and hearts. If we want a new awareness of Christ's birth tonight, we might give attention to those times when our heart skips, a knot lumps in our throat, and when feeling pulses through our veins. Here, right in the middle of it all, is where Christ is born.

Why not do away with the stable? Doing away with the stable might shatter some of our fantasies and fairy tales, but it would make a difference in how we view the Incarnation.

If Jesus, on the other hand, was born like all other peasant children, the event of his birth becomes something very positive and powerful. It means that Jesus is one of us. It means that God is present in the events and lives of ordinary people.

When we have been possessed by the understanding that God surfaces in the commonplace, then we are never the same again. When we understand that God goes to any lengths to meet us in the "stuff" of life, then we know that we can never hide from God. To see God as absent from the "stuff" of life is to deny the Incarnation.

On Christmas Eve more than any night of the year, we know that the God of the Christian faith is not on the boundary of life. He is Emmanuel—"God with us." If we open our ears tonight we can hear the God who has no voice and yet who speaks in everything that is—and who most of all speaks in the depths of our own being. We are the words of God.

Chapter Six **Christmas Day**

[Naomi] said, "See, your sister-in-law has gone back to her people and to her gods; return after your sister-in-law." But Ruth said, "Entreat me not to leave you or to return from following you; for where you go I will go, and where you lodge I will lodge; your people shall be my people, and your God my God; where you die I will die, and there I will be buried. May the Lord do so to me and more also if even death parts me from you." And when Naomi saw that she was determined to go with her, she said no more.

—Ruth 1:15–18

When the angels went away from them into heaven, the shepherds said to one another, "Let us go over to Bethlehem and see this thing that has happened, which the Lord has made known to us." And they went with haste, and found Mary and Joseph, and the babe lying in a manger. And when they saw it they made known the saying which had been told them concerning this child; and all who heard it wondered at what the shepherds told them. But Mary kept all these things, pondering them in her heart. And the shepherds returned, glorifying and praising God for all they had heard and seen, as it had been told them.

—Luke 2:15–20

John Netherton

Christmas Day: # The Whisper of Christmas

Every Saturday morning my father would give me a crumpled, one-dollar bill so that my brother and I could view the afternoon movie at the Bristol movie theater. With that one dollar I would buy two tickets, two bags of popcorn, two Nehi grape drinks, and two oversized, red jawbreakers. When my brother and I got home, my dad would say, "Put the change on the table." Those were big afternoons on what we now consider a very small amount of money.

Thirty long years have gone by since those days, and I have only faint memories of the "Bristol Picture Show," as we called it. I do not remember much about its color scheme, design, or floor plan. But I do remember the unforgettable smell of its popcorn. Every square inch of the run-down theater was filled with the aroma. Though I cannot recall much about the building, I can still remember the smell of that hot, buttery, salty popcorn.

My brother and I would chomp on that over-buttered popcorn while watching the Western. Every Saturday afternoon the story ended in the same predictable way. Regardless of the characters, the plot, the intrigue, or the strength of the antagonist, I knew with great certainty that the good guys were going to beat the bad guys. As the plot thickened and rethickened, I knew that the good guys were going to use their fast horses, smoking guns, and their scheming ingenuity to drive the mean antagonist out of those gold rush towns.

In moments of fantasy, I have wondered if God ever watched the Westerns. And, if so, why doesn't

God operate like Roy Rogers, Gene Autry, and Hopalong Cassidy? Why doesn't God use his power, influence, ingenuity, and might to drive the evil out of the world? Why doesn't God maneuver so that the good guys win over the bad guys, so that right is triumphant over wrong, and so that evil is driven out of the world?

Christmas, unlike the Westerns, tells a different kind of story. It tells us that God doesn't come to us like a hero. The narratives of this season tell us that God comes not as a predictable hero but in strange and unpredictable ways.

Our hunger for the predictable and the familiar is one of the reasons that we so enjoy this special time of the year. The longing is real because we have such a difficult time adjusting to a world that is increasingly unfamiliar. It is a welcome relief to be surrounded by the familiar once more: the fragrance of the old kitchen, the hanging of sentimental ornaments, the setting out of the familiar creche, listening to favorite carols, and observing the rituals that our families have followed for many, many years. Christmas and the days before and after present us with the opportunity to soak ourselves in the familiar. Now, for a time, we can flee from this increasingly strange and alien world of ours.

But if we understand the message of Christmas we cannot settle back into the tried and proven. The spirit and meaning of Christmas will not let us do that. There is something unsettling, unfamiliar, and shattering about the way God comes to us at this season of the year. That God comes in irregular ways is one of the mysteries of the Christmas story.

God's coming in this tiny infant is strange—really strange. It does not seem strange to us because we view the story as people who stand in the Christian tradition. Over the years we have "prettied up" the story. In the telling and retelling of the tale we have domesticated, decorated, and sentimentalized God's coming. What really happened in the hill town of Bethlehem has been covered up with a multitude of parking lot pageants, tired dramas, and almost silly attempts to display the narrative. The commonplace attempts of modern people to tell the story of Christ's birth have hidden the strangeness of it all. That which John the Baptist announced is still true: "Among you stands one whom you do not know" (John 1:26).

In *The Hungering Dark*, Frederick Buechner speaks of God's strangeness as vulgarity.

> The vulgarity of a God who adorns the sky at sunrise and sundown with colors no decent painter would dream of placing together... the vulgarity of a God who created a world full of hybrids like us—half ape, half human—and who keeps breaking back into the muck of this world. The vulgarity of a God who was born into a cave among hicks and the steaming dung of beasts only to grow up and die on a cross between crooks.

In *Oh, God!*—a delightful movie—God (George Burns) appears to Jerry (John Denver), the grocery clerk, as a customer. Here God is pictured as a little man in canvas shoes, checkered shirt, baggy pants, thick glasses, and a rather cute little cap. George Burns, portraying God, relates, moves, inspires, loves, and calls others to faith. The screenplay, like the Gospels, calls us to believe in a God who comes through unlikely people.

Those people in the movie who do not believe are those who need proof because God is not otherworldly and supernatural enough. The confused characters in the film are conditioned to look for God in only conventional ways. The people most irate about the claims that Burns is God are those who should know—a few theologians and a Bible-thumping evangelist.

God comes to us in unusual ways and through strange people. The story of Ruth in the Old Testament bears witness to the same theme.

A great and devastating famine came to Judah, forcing Elimelech to pick up his belongings and his family for a move to greener pastures in the land of Moab. Though it was but a few miles from Judah to Moab, the journey represented a monumental undertaking for a man to move his family and all that they possessed. It required packing animals and walking dusty hill roads. It required planning and risking. Most of all, the move meant relocating into a new culture.

Soon after Elimelech, his wife Naomi, and their two sons had settled down in the neighboring culture, Elimelech died, leaving Naomi to rear her two sons in a strange land. Here we have a Jewish widow, living away from her kin and outside of her beloved Judah, trying to rear two sons in a foreign environment. Her life became even more complicated when her Israelite sons grew to manhood and took for themselves Moabite women as their wives. For ten years the wives of these young men, Ruth and Orpah, lived with Naomi and her two sons. Then, as circumstances would have it, Naomi's two sons died, leaving the widow Naomi with two widowed daughters-in-law.

In due time the word came to Naomi that the famine had passed in Judah. Upon hearing that word, Naomi began to yearn for her homeland. Ruth and Orpah walked with her to the border that separated Judah from Moab. As they walked, Naomi advised her daughters-in-law to remain in their homeland and to seek husbands. Orpah heeded

Naomi's advice, gave her a loving kiss, and returned to her people.

Ruth, however, "clave" to her mother-in-law and begged to go with her to Judah. Willing to leave her people, culture, and customs, she said:

> Entreat me not to leave thee, or to return from following after thee: for whither thou goest, I will go; and where thou lodgest, I will lodge; thy people shall be my people and thy God my God: Where thou diest, I will die, and there will I be buried: the Lord do so to me, and more also, if ought but death part thee and me.
>
> —Ruth 1:16–17, KJV

These words are the story of a soul's conversion. They beautifully tell about a Moabite girl who took the people and God of Israel as her own. Something is taken away from these words when they are used at weddings because they were not spoken between a man and woman, but between a young woman and her mother-in-law.

Ruth and Naomi found their way to Bethlehem where Ruth noticed Boaz, a wealthy land owner. It was impossible to believe that anything could come of that relationship. He was Jewish. She was a heathen Moabite. He was rich. She was poor. He owned land. She gleaned barley from his land. He was a kinsman of Elimelech. She was related by marriage. He was filled with the culture and customs of Judah. She knew only the ways of Moab. He had known one lifestyle. She had known another. In spite of all the limitations and obstacles, they fell in love with each other. No one thought it would work. It seemed improbable that such great differences could be reconciled.

Late one winter afternoon I was in my study when a quiet knock sounded through the windowless door which separated my office from the hall. When I opened the door, I found a young man dressed in a dark and well-tailored suit and a young woman clad in a simple print dress. "We want to talk with a minister," they said. I invited them to sit across from my writing desk in two overstuffed rocking chairs.

After exchanging some light conversation, they told me why they had come. They were both students at a nearby university where they had met. They had been dating for over a year and had decided to marry. They were different. He was the son of a prominent banker. She was the daughter of a baker. He lived with his family in a lovely, two-story house. Her family lived in a humble cottage near the railroad. His family was large, influential, and professional. Working, blue-collar people made up her clan. Because of their apparent differences, both families opposed the marriage. Neither family knew that she was pregnant. The young couple feared further rejection, so they had not told their families about the baby.

After pondering their story, I decided to officiate for their wedding. Never will I forget that marriage service! He came to the church in that same dark suit. She had washed and ironed that same print dress. A few friends attended. The parents of both elected not to come. Just before the wedding was to begin, he asked if a friend could play the guitar for the processional. Reluctantly I consented.

Wearing blue jeans, the long-haired friend strode out to the front of the sanctuary, threw his skinny leg over the front pew, and started picking the song, "Bridge Over Troubled Waters." Everything in my proper seminary training mitigated against that approach to the service of marriage, but I choked back my feelings and proceeded with the service.

While reading the service I had the gnawing feeling that this marriage could never work. She was expecting. There was no parental support. The cultures and backgrounds were vastly different. They answered the questions and nervously held hands because there was no ring to exchange. I pronounced them husband and wife and they went on their way. There was nothing to shout about. Only a whisper seemed appropriate.

Several years later I received a letter in the mail. "You probably will not remember us," the letter read, "but you officiated at our wedding about six years ago. I was pregnant, our parents did not come to the service, and you let one of our friends play the guitar for the wedding march." The memory of that occasion flooded across my mind as my eyes scanned the lines like one searching for something special. The epistle continued: "I just wanted to write and tell you that my husband recently graduated from medical school and that we are having our second child baptized at a nearby church tomorrow. We are seriously considering short term missionary service. I have never told you this, but I now want to say that when everyone was against us, the church stood by us. How grateful we are." How grateful I was! In spite of all the differences, love had its birth and flowered in the lives of those two people.

And so it was with Boaz and Ruth. No one thought it would work. But God worked through their relationship to accomplish his purpose. According to the Book of Ruth, Boaz and Ruth had a son whose name was Obed who became the father of Jesse who was the father of David... and Jesus, as we know, was born of the house and lineage of David.

Ruth and Boaz and that young couple who came to my office are examples of how God uses the unexpected to triumph over human obstacles to fulfill his purpose. God's ends are often fulfilled in irregular ways and according to methods which seem strange and foreign.

Christmas is a time when we understand that God's way is often more like the whisper than the shout.

When something very special is to be spoken, it is often said with a whisper. Upon receiving a significant gift the receiver whispers, "Thank you." After experiencing a magnificent symphony, the audience will whisper its approval before breaking forth into thundering applause. Indeed, the most important moments of life are shared with a hushed tone.

When a man first tells a woman of his love for her, he does not shout, "I LOVE YOU." Instead he quietly and gently whispers, "I love you." She returns his love not with clapping or yelling but with an almost inaudible whisper.

In the stories, meanings, and symbols of life, God often whispers to humankind. From the foretellings of the Old Testament until the birth of an innocent, vulnerable baby, God whispered his profound love for people. Christmastide and Epiphany, more than any other time of the year, are seasons of God's whispering love. In the Word made flesh, God does not holler at us. No! In the birth of this babbling child in a Bethlehem manger, God speaks gently, softly, and quietly.

Our society, unfortunately, wants to shout about Christmastide. Boisterous parties, banging parades, jangling TV commercials, ear-bursting music seem unlike the whisper of God's way.

One of the reasons that the Christmas carol "Silent Night" is so universal in its popularity is that it almost whispers about the birth. Sing it loudly and its meaning will be violated. The softer it is sung, the closer one comes to the richness and depth of its meaning.

God has a wonderful way of avoiding redundancy. No snowflake is geometrically the same as any other snowflake; no person's fingerprint matches any other's; no set of genes is assembled in the exact order of any other arrangement of genes. God, likewise, comes in many ways. But no way is more powerful than the whisper of an innocent baby.

The whisper, not the shout, is God's grammar of love for most of life.

**First Week after
Christmas**

Now when Jesus was born in Bethlehem of
Judea in the days of Herod the king, behold, wise
men from the East came to Jerusalem, saying,
"Where is he who has been born king of the
Jews? For we have seen his star in the East, and
have come to worship him." When Herod the king
heard this, he was troubled, and all Jerusalem with
him; and assembling all the chief priests and
scribes of the people, he inquired of them where
the Christ was to be born. They told him, "In
Bethlehem of Judea...." Then Herod summoned the
wise men secretly and ascertained from them what
time the star appeared; and he sent them to Bethlehem, saying, "Go and search diligently for the
child, and when you have found him bring me
word, that I too may come and worship him." When
they had heard the king they went their way; and
lo, the star which they had seen in the East went
before them, till it came to rest over the place
where the child was. When they saw the star, they
rejoiced exceedingly with great joy; and going into
the house they saw the child with Mary his mother.
and they fell down and worshiped him. Then, open-
ing their treasures, they offered him gifts, gold and
frankincense and myrrh. And being warned in a
dream not to return to Herod, they departed to their
own country by another way.

—Matthew 2:1–12

Robert Reddig

Sunday: Responding to Christ's Birth

Telling the story of Christ's birth is not enough for Matthew! He also told about two reactions to the birth of the Messiah.

The first reaction, as Matthew told it, was from the magi who came from the East to Jerusalem asking the question, "Where is the newborn king of the Jews?" Contemporary customs, children dressed in faded bathrobes, tired Christmas pageants, and unsightly stable scenes on church parking lots have taken away from the wisdom in the wise men's story.

It is difficult to understand what Matthew meant by *magi*. They might have been Zoroastrian priests who had special power to interpret dreams. Or possibly men who practiced various forms of secret love and magic. In the Old Testament they were referred to as enchanters, astronomers, and interpreters of dreams and visionary messages. In early first century Rome they were known as astrologers, magicians, and readers of dreams. In Acts 8:9–24, Luke tells the story of Simon, a magus in Samaria who amazed everyone with his magical powers; later, Acts 13:6–11 tells of Bar-Jesus, a Jewish magus and false prophet on the island of Cyprus. Therefore the term *magi* refers to a large number of people engaged in occult arts. It also covers a wide range of astronomers, fortune-tellers, priestly augurs, and wandering magicians. Since Matthew depicts the magi as having seen a star, it is highly possible that they were astrologers from beyond Palestine.

In the Old Testament the "people of the East"

107

were also desert Arabs. These nomadic Arabs often had wise men as a natural part of their envoy. First Kings 5:12 and Proverbs 30:1 and 31:1 refer to the wisdom that was commonly associated with these wise men. Likewise astrology was not unknown to the Arabs, and Arabian tribes often took their names from the stars. In addition, gold, frankincense, and myrrh were gifts that Eastern Arabs would use to express their feelings.

According to Matthew, these Arab astrologers reacted to the birth of Jesus by following a star to the city of Jerusalem, a scant five miles from the hill town of Bethlehem. After making inquiry as to the birthplace of Jesus, they followed the star to Bethlehem where they found the child and Mary, his mother.

Having found the infant, they bowed down and paid him homage and then they opened their treasure boxes and brought out gifts of gold, frankincense, and myrrh. For centuries people have speculated about the meaning of these gifts. In each special gift there are rich symbolism and deep meaning for, in the gifts they brought, one sees the wisdom of the magi.

Thankfully the Arab astrologers did not bring the child a toy, a silver spoon, or a teething ring. Nor did they bring a cute little outfit for his circumcision. Nor did they bring clothing or flowers for the mother. They brought gifts which expressed their hope for the Christ child.

One of the treasure boxes contained gold which was the king of metals because the wise men wanted Jesus to be the "King of kings." The ancient writer Seneca said that one should never approach a king without the gift of gold. So the gift of gold was presented because the astrologers wanted Bethlehem's babe to become the Lord of life.

The rule of Jesus, as we know, did not unfold like many had expected. In fact the rule of Jesus was a complete reversal of what the world expected from its kings. He ruled not with power, but with love. Self-surrender and service were his methods. His rule expressed itself as he became a friend to hated tax collectors, flagrant sinners, the forgotten poor, and the misunderstood outcast. The gift of gold should serve as a constant reminder to us that we have been identified by a Lord whose power is rooted in love and self-surrender.

Frankincense, an aromatic gum resin used for incense by the priests, was brought as the middle gift. There is the possibility that these traveling wise men wanted the baby to become like a priest who used the frankincense. The chief role of a priest is to build bridges between God and people. The wise men wanted the son of God to be a bridge builder. They wanted him to be the bridge which would connect God to all people and people to each other.

The New Testament speaks about a Jesus who spent himself building bridges not barriers. Those who are marked as his followers are also called to be priests or bridge builders for each other. The church, by its very essence, is called to build bridges between black and white, the rich and poor, the Western centers of power and the Third World, the "haves" and the "have nots," and wherever separations appear in the life of humanity. The church that is not bringing people together in community is simply not being the church of Jesus Christ. The will of God is being done when people are fashioned into communities of mutual love and respect.

The third gift box contained myrrh, used in the ancient world to embalm the dead and as a symbol of suffering. These Gentile astrologers wanted their

Messiah to be the kind of Lord who would suffer for his people. They did not want a Christ who would dodge a cross, be protected from the hurts of humanity, or fail to identify with the lonely and alienated. They wanted a Saviour who would suffer for and take upon himself the sufferings of humanity.

According to the Gospels, Jesus lived up to that which was symbolized by myrrh because he was glorified through his passion, death, and resurrection. The real church, the genuine community of believers, exists wherever and whenever people of faith enter into the sufferings of humanity as did Jesus.

The gifts could also be symbols relating to different aspects of the Christian's response to the Messiah's birth: gold symbolizing virtue, incense symbolizing prayer, and myrrh symbolizing suffering.

The believer does not respond to the birth of the Christ child in a vacuum, or with an overdose of ceremony, or with empty words, or with false deeds. Most Christians react to Christ's birth by displaying a life filled with good deeds. "By this my Father is glorified," said Jesus, "that you bear much fruit" (John 15:8). Not to bear good fruit is to be distant from the spirit of the living Christ. Good deeds are indeed the gold of the Christian's life.

Nor can the Christian be fed for the journey without prayer. Prayer is that resource which helps us to practice the presence of Christ in every relationship of life. Rufus M. Jones in *The Double Search* puts it this way:

It is a primary truth of Christianity that God reaches us directly. No person is insulated. As ocean floods the inlets, as sunlight environs the plant, so God enfolds and enwreathes the finite spirit. There is this difference, however, inlet and plant are penetrated whether they will or not. Sea and sunshine crowd

themselves in *a tergo.* Not so with God. He can be
received only through doors that are *purposely* opened
for him. A person may live as near God as the bubble
is to the ocean and yet not find him. He may be
"closer than breathing, nearer than hands or feet,"
and still be missed. Historical Christianity is dry and
formal when it lacks the immediate and inward response to our Great Companion; but our spirits are
trained to know him, to appreciate him, by the medi-
ation of historical revelation. A person's spiritual life
is always dwarfed when cut apart from history. Mysti-
cism is empty unless it is enriched by outward and
historical revelation. The supreme education of the
soul comes through an intimate acquaintance with
Jesus Christ of history.

Likewise, the symbol of myrrh continues to call
the Christian to live a life of passion. Today it
appears that a passion for life itself is disappearing.
Many fear that the world will end in atomic death.
Others expect ecological death. It seems to me that
we will come to ruin long before that by means of
our own apathy. The worst thing is that too many of
us have gotten used to it. Just as we have become
accustomed to crime in our big cities, so we have
become accustomed to the threat of death through
nuclear weapons and to the destruction of our
environment. We will become accustomed to death
even before it comes. Why? Because when the pas-
sionate devotion to life is missing, the powers to
resist evil are paralyzed. Therefore if we want to live
today, we must consciously will life. We must learn
to love life with such a passion that we no longer
become accustomed to the powers of destruction.
We must overcome our own apathy and be seized by
the passion for life.

To follow as a disciple means to share in both
the joy and the suffering of humanity. Christ's peo-

ple are concerned about the joy and the hurt of life but neither one to the exclusion of the other. Good news and passion are linked together in this faith and there can be no gospel without passion. As one travels in "The Way" one gradually understands that the gospel, as symbolized by myrrh, must have a passion as well as a success.

A central concept that Matthew wanted to convey is that some reacted to the birth of Jesus with acceptance and devotion. He does this by showing that the first to pay homage to the newborn King of the Jews were Gentiles from the East. In these magi Matthew anticipated all of those who would respond to Christ's birth by paying homage.

Woven into this touching story of the magi's devotion is the parable of Herod's reaction to the birth of the King of the Jews. Herod responded to the birth not by paying homage, but by plotting to kill the child. Therein lies a paradox: Herod, the chief priests, and the scribes—people who have the scriptures and can plainly see what the prophets have said—are not willing to worship the newborn king. Thus we have a twofold reaction to the birth of Christ. The wise men of the Gentiles accept and pay homage but the ruler of Jerusalem and all the chief priests and scribes of the people do not believe. Rather, they conspire against the King of the Jews and seek to put him to death.

It is not difficult to understand why Herod responded as he did. His kingdom was threatened by the possibility of a new king. The possibility of being displaced did not bring him great joy. Instead it brought fear. If this child was truly the Messiah, it would alter all that Herod believed to be important.

In *The Gospel in Solentiname*, Ernesto Cardenal reports that after reading Matthew 2, a Nicaraguan farm worker responded by saying: "I think these wise

men (fouled) things up when they went to Herod
asking about a liberator. It would be like someone
going to Somoza now to ask him where's the man
who's going to liberate Nicaragua."

Whenever and wherever the message of Christ
is taken into the world there is the possibility that it
will be met with rejection. I was a pastor in Memphis,
Tennessee, when Dr. Martin Luther King, Jr. was
shot while standing on the balcony of a downtown
motel. I learned of the shooting when our black
custodian interrupted the finance committee meeting by shouting, "Dr. King has been shot, Dr. King
has been shot!" The next morning's issue of *The
Commercial Appeal,* our local newspaper, urgently
called the clergy of the city to a meeting.

Pastors representing every racial, cultural, and
educational level in the city gathered for a mass
meeting which had been called by the bold head-
lines of the city newspaper. Reverend James Lawson,
a friend of Dr. King's and an effective pastor in
South Memphis, read the Old Testament lesson.
The local Greek Orthodox priest read from the New
Testament and symbolically kissed the feet of Mr.
Lawson. Reverend Frank McRae, a courageous leader in the United Methodist Church, spoke about
hope in the midst of despair.

After a session of Bible study, prayer, and speaking the clergy decided to march *en masse* to the office
of Mayor Henry Loeb, as a symbol of love and
reconciliation. We wanted the Mayor to reconsider
his opposition to the striking sanitation workers as
a symbol of repentance and love.

After leaving the sanctuary, we formed ourselves
in lines two abreast and started walking toward the
city hall. Just before we had completed one block of
our march, a young deacon from St. Mary's ran
back into the church and brought out the proces-

sional cross which was commonly used on Sunday morning for the worship service. With humility and yet boldness, he put himself at the head of the processional now aimed at the city's seat of power. As we walked, television cameras descended upon us. Reporters from New York to California started pumping us with questions about our motives and how we felt about what had happened the night before.

When our journey was about half completed, an older woman started yelling from a second floor apartment window. Because of the traffic, the cameras, the reporters, and the noise her speech was, at first, inaudible. As I drew closer to her flowerboxed window, I could hear the anger of her shrill voice: "The cross belongs in the church! The cross belongs in the church! I am a member of St. Mary's. Take the cross back to the church where it belongs." Her secure kingdom, like Herod's, was being threatened. And she responded not with homage but with rejection.

The message of Jesus often brings peace, but it also brings trouble. Even in our contemporary society, Christ's message of love, justice, and peace invades our kingdoms of selfishness, pride, power, injustice, and provincialism. The Herods continue to stalk the world trying to discover ways to silence the message. In our modern world there are evil forces which tirelessly attempt to silence the message which was in Christ.

Those who have responded to the revelation of God in Christ instinctively know that rejection is possible. As H. Richard Niebuhr notes in *The Meaning of Revelation*:

> When we speak of revelation...we mean rather that something has happened which compels our faith

and which requires us to seek rationality and unity in the whole of our history. Revelation is like the kingdom of God.... The Kingdom proves itself to be the kingdom of God not only by its immediate worth but also by its instrumental value in leading to secondary goods, and revelation proves itself to be revelation of reality not only by its intrinsic verity, but also by its ability to guide people to many other truths.

Disciples of Jesus, having been led to "many other truths," can expect both affirmation and rejection.

Therefore there are two reactions to the appearance of the Messiah: homage and rejection. It is too easy and clean to say that some respond by giving as did the magi while others react by opposing the meaning of Christ's birth as did Herod. Not one person reading these words is entirely like the magi. Nor is any reader exactly like Herod. We are, at best, a mixture of the devotion and denial. We are neither one nor the other, but an uneasy mixture of both.

Many country music artists understand the dual nature which exists within humankind. While on stage, the country musician can sing about sex, lust, cheating, gambling, and unfaithfulness and then close the program by singing "Amazing Grace." The contradiction is shockingly apparent but ever so typical of how we really are.

What happens on the country music stage is a microcosm of what much of our life is like. For six days in every week we live sinful, broken lives and then sing the hymns of faith with great feeling on the following Sunday morning. In spite of the hell we have either created or been through, we flock to Christmas Eve services with faith welling up within. In spite of the alienation and despair we either cause or experience, we insist upon attaching our-selves to the community of believers.

Frederick Buechner says in *Telling the Truth:*

> Joy happens, to use Tolkien's word, and the fairy tale where it happens is not a world where everything is sweetness and light. It is not Disney Land where everything is kept spotless. . . . On the contrary, the world where this Joy happens is as full of darkness as our own world, and that is why when it happens it is as poignant as grief and can bring tears to our eyes. It can bring tears to our eyes because it might so easily not have happened.

Today marks the first Sunday after Christmas, often the most undervalued celebration of the Chris-tian year. It is this day which proclaims the purpose of the Incarnation: the manifestation of God through Christ to the world. As Chrysostom preached in A.D. 386, "Up to this day he (Jesus) was unknown to the multitudes."

In this season of manifestation we are drawn to understand that God is revealed to both the Herods and the Gentile Arab astrologers. The revelation of God is up to God and not to us. But one of the things that makes this time such a day of unbridled celebration is precisely the nature of God. It is God's nature to come to us, to search us out, to meet us on the journey, to make Godself known to us. It is God's nature not to be known by a few people, but by the multitudes. God yearns to be known. God is an encountering God, and that is the reason the Wise Men found Jesus. They responded in the mo-ment and they were led where they were beckoned. They were willing to look for the king in unlikely places. What they found was a surprise. Expecting to find a future king, they encountered a living God.

Having experienced the living God, they returned home by a different route. If we have really experienced God during these days of Christmas, we will return home as different people who travel by a different way.

Daily Reflections

Monday: Behind the Labels

He owned the only two-story building in my childhood, blue-collar neighborhood. It was a dusty, red brick affair which housed a barber shop, a drug store, and his dry goods store on the street level. Upstairs there were a smoke-filled pool hall and a dance studio. I knew they were upstairs because the scribbled sign said so, not because I was permitted to go. My parents and my religion forbade such pursuits into the land of indecency.

The owner was more interesting than the building and its occupants. His short, chubby, box-like body was covered by thick black hair which framed his distinctively Jewish facial features. His name escapes me. The husky sound of his accented voice does not. He was an oddity for our neck-of-the-woods. Not only did he own the only two-story edifice, he was our solo Jew. We did not know him but we had a bushel full of stereotypes for him. Almost everyone from the river to the railroad had a derogatory name for this man whom we did not know.

My daughters have had a different experience. They have Jewish friends who invite them to Bar Mitzvahs. They have played the Jewish games, attended worship at the Temple, sung Hebrew songs, and visited in Jewish homes. My daughters do not use the derogatory words that rolled across my youthful tongue. Their relationships have given them a different feeling and perception. If I had known that

Jewish store owner, I probably would have had a different feeling.

The truth is that when we call other people by prejudging names it says more about us than it does them. If we knew the persons behind the labels, we would probably feel more compassionate and less judgmental. To know one another is to increase the possibility of love. Not to know one another is to increase the possibility of discord. Knowing one another will not solve all of our problems, but it will allow us to be accepting of one another while being free to disagree over principles.

> We love, because he first loved us. If anyone says, "I love God," and hates his brother, he is a liar; for he who does not love his brother whom he has seen, cannot love God whom he has not seen. And this commandment we have from him, that he who loves God should love his brother also.
>
> —1 John 4:19–21

The love which came down at Christmas is a love that beckons us not to isolation but to community.

Tuesday: Two Responses

Possibly he was broke. Who knows. Maybe he did not want to make the long trek back through the house to fetch his wallet. The cause might not have appealed to him. His house was new, large, pretentious, and expensive.

A group from our youth fellowship went to his door to sing carols. They sang four carols and then said they were taking a collection for the day-care center. Anxiously they waited for his response. For singing four carols, getting out in the bitter cold for children who need a day home, this individual, for whatever reason, put six pennies in the outstretched hand of a young person.

When the youth came back to our house for cookies and hot chocolate, they were brimming full with the story about the man who gave six cents. They laughed at him, imitated him, cautiously scolded him, and questioned how anyone could do such a thing. I said to a few of the youth, "Did anyone appreciate your coming?" "Oh, yes," they replied. "Some people thanked us and wanted us to stay longer, and one lady even gave us a whole plate of cookies. We got a bunch of compliments and Merry Christmases."

I hope that our youth learned that whenever one works for a good cause there are many levels of response. Some respond with six cents and others with generosity.

That's the way it was with the Messiah's birth. Some received it with gladness and joy while others gave scant heed.

Wednesday: The Fringes of Time

One Sunday I talked about God's gift of time. How we kill it. How we need to take it. How time gives us both ice cream and spinach and hills and valleys. How time is a gift and how we should, as with talents, money, and service be good stewards of it. At best it was just a plain, vanilla sermon not worthy of any honorable mention. While shaking hands, a member of the congregation thoughtfully said, "What about the fringes of time?" There was something that the sermon had not considered—the bits and pieces of time.

The coming year will not yield us huge chunks of time to do with as we please. It is unrealistic to expect that! But the next twelve months will give us many opportunities to use, not use, or misuse the fringes of time. To use wisely the fragments of time might just make a significant difference in the quality of this year.

If we would, on occasion, use the fringes for reflection and meditation, we might discover that the mystery of life has a face with a name. The name of that face for me is Christ.

Could it be that Christ reveals himself to us on the fringes as well as in the midst of our busy lives?

Thursday: Depression

The feeling of depression is not uncommon during this season. This season, like no other, causes us to reflect and remember. Some of those memories are painful. For those who have experienced a move to a far away city, the death of a loved one, divorce, loneliness, or moral failure and broken relationships these days can be filled with depression. "Feeling down" is familiar to many people.

English author Evelyn Waugh wrote a novel based on his own depressive experience, *The Ordeal of Gilbert Pinfold.* In that novel he reminded us that everybody knows depression in its milder and heavier forms because we all experience a loss, a death, or a separation from a loved one. Therein lies at least one cause of depression.

Depression also tells us that we are limited, finite, and that we are dependent upon God and others for help. Depression will not let us forget that we need receptivity, patience, and a great willingness on the part of someone to understand our depressed pattern of life.

A feeling of depression often intrudes into the days that follow Christmas because we experience a moving away or separation from a joyous season. At times this depression is acute because others have not lived up to our expectations during Advent and Christmas.

In spite of our feeling of loss and separation, the message of the Incarnation is clear: we are not separated from God nor are we lost to God's will.

Friday: A Way Out

I recently had the privilege of going with a fifth and sixth grade math class to experience the movie, *Gandhi.* The entire theater had been booked by a local middle school. It was filled with alert, wiggling children who had the ability to talk faster than they could wiggle.

Just before the show started one little chap sidled up to me and said, "Mr. Pennel, may I borrow a dime?" "Sure," I replied, "is that enough?" "Yep," he whispered, "that will do." He disappeared into the crowd of youngsters who filled every inch of the aisle. Just before the curtain parted, he came back with a bucket of popcorn that was so large he could scarcely get his arms around it and enough Coke to float his math book. I was so interested in his groceries that I went out to the concession stand and found that his refreshments totaled a whopping $3.50. That lad ought to be in the White House Cabinet because he either knows how to stretch a dime or borrow thirty-five of them.

As the film got started, I soon forgot about the little boy who had borrowed a dime. I was touched by Gandhi and the principle for which he stood. For three hours I was in touch with that which is beyond and yet within. In that film one is able to experience the highest teachings of the Christian faith reduced to a little, brown, non-Christian man from India. The forces that sought to silence Gandhi are the same evil forces which sought to silence Jesus and many of his followers.

When the movie was over, I moved slowly down our row and toward the aisle. The lad was gone, his popcorn half eaten and his Coke half drunk. Had he learned that Gandhi gave the world a way out and that humankind failed to take it, or did he simply enjoy the pop and corn?

Are we so busy enjoying the refreshments this holiday season that we fail to see that the birth of Christ has offered the world a way out?

Saturday: Unfinished

The remarkable feature of Schubert's *Unfinished Symphony* is that it sounds altogether like a finished product to the ears of the average listener. Yet we know that Schubert's symphony, however exquisite and meaningful in itself, is still unfinished. To be a symphony a work must have four movements, and this has only two. Indeed, the true greatness of what he has already written lies not in its own intrinsic worth and beauty, but in its promise of the exciting climactic variations that would normally follow.

The *Unfinished Symphony* is great for its own sake, but its true greatness lies in that to which it points. Indeed, it points beyond itself to an infinite mystery which cannot be captured by any finite expression.

The church has the opportunity to keep alive the mystery of how God is revealed. During Advent we can point to the mystery, but we cannot explain it.

Advent leads to Christmas and the story of Emmanuel is yet to be finished.

The author, Joe E. Pennel, Jr., is Senior Minister of Belmont United Methodist Church in Nashville, Tennessee. Dr. Pennel holds a Doctorate of the Ministry degree from Vanderbilt Divinity School in Nashville. He has contributed articles to The *Christian Home, Accent on Youth,* and *Pulpit Digest,* as well as preparing *A Connectional Community* which was published by Abingdon Press.